DEBRA HOSSEINI

Consulting Editors
Keri Bowers
Kurt Muzikar
Nancy Lea Speer

Design
Debra Hosseini

Cover Design
Debra Hosseini

Cover Artists
Justin Canha: "Boy Eating Corn," Kevin Hosseini: "Gauguin & Me,"
Christian Early: "Crazy Lady in Yellow," Seth Chwast: "Self Study in Blue/Green"

Back Cover Artists
These four art selections have been chosen by the United Nations
for stamps to commemorate 2012 World Autism Day
Seth Chwast: "Mythical Creatures (Panel 1),"
Trent Altman: "An Abstract Flower Garden II,"
Ryan Smoluk: "The Path," J.A. Tan: "Victory"

End Pages
Frank Louis Allen - front: "War on Bruce Springsteen"
Frank Louis Allen - back: "Hipster Wars"

The Art of Autism website: www.the-art-of-autism.com
P.O. Box 630
Carpinteria, CA 93014
Email: theartofautism@gmail.com

10 9 8 7 6 5 4 3 2 1   First Edition

This edition © 2012 Debra Hosseini
All rights reserved.

ISBN 978-0-9839834-0-8
Library of Congress Control Number: 2012902623

First Trademark Edition, 2012

Printed in the USA through Bolton Associates, Inc. San Rafael, CA 94901

No part of this publication may be reproduced in any form without permission. Every effort has been made to trace accurate ownership of copyrighted text and visual materials. Errors or ommissions will be corrected in subsequent editions. Please note many individuals on the autism spectrum use language in novel and creative ways. We've made every effort to retain the authenticity of each writer's unique voice.

"What would happen if the autism gene was eliminated from the gene pool? "You would have a bunch of people standing around in a cave, chatting and socializing and not getting anything done."
　　　　Temple Grandin, *The Way I See It: A Personal Look at Autism and Asperger's*

J.A. Tan   *Victory*   2012 United Nations World Autism Day stamp selection

"One young boy negotiating the world in a way he knows. One young boy listening to a different tune as he makes sense of the world around. Not an easy task as he perceives the world differently from others. He is met with confused looks, angry looks, disturbed looks, happy looks, questioning looks…so many questions but no one answer. Yet this young boy continues on his journey never giving up…until…

"Supported by his immediate family - all five of them always a strong presence in his life - friends, and professionals this young boy today has claimed victory over the many challenges of his life. Today, with happy faces around him he shows the world the 'victory' of an artist with autism achieved with patience, discipline, perseverance, love, and a positive attitude."

J.A. Tan

CONTENTS

- 6   THE ART OF AUTISM: SHIFTING PERCEPTIONS
  Debra Hosseini

- 8   PREFACE
  Keri Bowers

- 9   SELF-REFLECTIONS

- 29   THE JOURNEY

- 30   MYTHS, AUTISM AND THE ARTIST
  Darold Treffert, M.D.

- 45   PATTERNS

- 46   THE IMPORTANCE OF ART AND MUSIC
  Stephen Shore, Ed.D.

- 61   THE PROCESS

- 62   AT SOCIETY'S GROWING EDGE
  Colin Zimbleman, Ph.D.

- 81   CONNECTIONS

- 93   FEELINGS & EMOTIONS

- 94   THE CREATIVE POTENTIAL OF THOSE ON THE SPECTRUM
  Rebecca McKenzie, Ph.D.

- 111   PASSIONS

- 127   HOPE

- 128   IT TAKES A CHILD
  Elaine Hall

- 142   THANK YOU

- 143   INDEX OF ARTISTS

- 144   ORGANIZATIONS THAT SUPPORT ARTISTS

The Art of Autism: Shifting Perceptions
Debra Hosseini

As I compiled this book of art, poetry, and stories, it occurred to me that the stories in the book are as amazing as the art. Many of the stories are about connections; connections between brother and brother, sister and brother, and parent and child. Many stories are about parents who have nurtured their child's creative spirit. Many are about people on the spectrum who have learned to work with their strengths and have used their unique perception of the world to create their art. All of the stories come from the heart.

The stories made me ponder. What if, with conscious effort and deliberation, a person's perceived "deficits" can be transformed into strengths? Hans Asperger suggested that those diagnosed with high-functioning autism tend to have "… a particular originality of thought and experience, which may well lead to exceptional achievements in later life." We now know the plasticity of the brain allows us to grow well beyond the formative years.

Seth Chwast, an artist in this book, experienced tremendous growth in his twenties. His hallmark line is "grow your brain." As you'll see in the stories that follow, other individuals with autism have remarkable breakthroughs well into their fifties.

It became apparent this book should be about shifting perceptions: recognizing and developing strengths; the power of family in nurturing individuality, creativity, and teaching life skills; the liberation late diagnosis offers some on the Asperger's spectrum; how alternative means of communication can assist those who have trouble with verbal expression; the sensory fulfillment experienced through the act of creation; as well as meaningful collaboration amongst like-minded organizations. These keys to shifting perceptions unlock resources within the autism community.

Recognizing and Developing Strengths

Each page illustrates the strengths of the artists, including: the ability to see patterns that are invisible to many others; the deep relationship many have with nature and animals; an acute spatial awareness, allowing some on the spectrum to know where they are, even in unfamiliar places, also assisting in determining the best medium to use in giving voice to their art on canvas; an innate gift to focus on an area of interest for extended periods of time; memory skills, allowing some to retain minute details of past events or places with astounding accuracy; acute sensitivities akin to extra-sensory perception and intuition; and novel and innovative uses of different mediums.

Their genius also lies in the transformation of annoying or compulsive behaviors, such as repetitive tearing of paper, into a form of art. Grant Manier's pages (p. 72-73) on eco-art show how his mom, Julie, helped him use his obsession with tearing paper to do just that.

The Importance of Family

Many of the artists have extremely supportive families who provide them with opportunities and resources to explore their creativity. Those families who have grown the most, are consistently the ones who move through their grief and shock of the initial diagnosis, to acceptance and embracing their child for whom they are. Many have strong belief systems and see their child as a gift.

Usually, one parent takes responsibility for finding and scheduling mentors, shipping the art, entering exhibitions, and creating a "buzz" around their child. Every single child with autism in this book, whose art has come to public light, has a parent or relative who recognized and promoted their talent. Some of these parents switched careers because of their children; others changed geographic locations of the family to better position their child's success.

Two artists in the book, Neri Avraham and J.A. Tan, have families who moved to different countries to provide better services and opportunities. The importance of family support can't be overemphasized. As art programs continue to be cut in our schools, the onus of providing exposure to the arts has fallen on the individual and their communities.

The Liberation of Late Diagnosis

Submissions were received from many adults recently diagnosed with Asperger's Syndrome. With the diagnosis comes a change in the way they perceive themselves. A freedom of self-expression is born from knowing they are not mentally ill. Some are also comforted knowing they are no longer alone. Frank Allen, Steven Selpal, Nekea Blakoev and Michael McManmon all speak of the liberation they experienced after discovering they have Asperger's.

Normally, a single label for an individual can be limiting, yet in the case of a diagnosis of Asperger's, the label helps the individual understand why aspects of their lives have been difficult and why their world views often seem to differ from the "norm." This realization presents a step toward greater self-awareness and growth both as a person and as an artist.

Alternate Means of Communication

Four of the artists and poets in the book use Facilitated Communication (FC) - the process of using a person who facilitates with a letter board or keyboard. This controversial technique gained international recognition when Tito Mukhopadhyay appeared on *Sixty Minutes* in the 1990's. Until recently, accounts of autism were limited to those who had verbal ability and writing skills. Through FC, poets such as Sydney Edmond, Louisa Jensen, and Craig Roveta can now share their world with the rest of us. Poet Louisa Jensen (p. 82) says, *"I've always wanted to help people understand that life for a nonverbal autistic person is not how it seems."*

FC has given teachers and caregivers reason to pause when making the assumption that nonverbal individuals on the spectrum lack intelligence or cognizance of what is happening.

Sensory Fulfillment

Many in the book talk about how the process of creating art or poetry fulfills a sensory need. Due to an intense desire to cut, to tear, to blend colors, to put sticks and other materials into their works, individuals on the autism spectrum are naturally drawn to their unique, preferred art form. See the chapter titled "The Process" (p. 61-80) for examples.

For my son, Kevin (p. 76-77), the palette knife has been a major tool in his creations. He likes the feel of the paint under the knife moving across the canvas. In earlier years, he liked to create a gooey mess on his palette, then scrape lumps of unused paint from the palette into a large jar and gleefully scoop up globs of this old paint, incorporating it into his work.

Poets use words in much the same manner. The fixation on words and groups of words, free association and alliteration, are means of fulfillment through self-expression.

The Importance of Collaboration

In 2011, Keri Bowers and I came together to create *The Art of Autism* collaborative. We are working together to create a kinder and more accepting society for all children. Organizations serving individuals with developmental disabilities need to work together. Sharing resources, opportunities, and knowledge are key to helping our children.

It does take a village.

Preface
Keri Bowers

Long before the advent of cities, agriculture, and writing, art thrived as an integrated and inseparable part of the human experience. Art has recorded our stories, traditions, history, and emotions. It is at the core of our individual and collective spiritual experiences and cannot be separated from who we are. Art reflects the advancements and declines of our cultures.

Russian painter, writer, and art theorist, Wassily Kandinsky once wrote "Every work of art is the child of its age and, in many cases, the mother of our emotions..."

And so it is with *The Art of Autism: Shifting Perceptions*.

A pivotal work of art itself, this book shows the genius and challenges of autism. Through the visions of the artists, the metaphoric child - born of the *Age of Autism* - teases our consciousness and shifts our notions of what it is to be autistic.

Where can the fragmented and often isolated autism community find common ground? Through the arts. The arts unite. Art is a mechanism which allows the artificial boundaries to melt - it's the way many in our population can connect. That is why this book included a chapter called *Connections*.

Reading this work is an experience unto itself, a metaphorical journey. The journey entails self-reflection, expression, finding an authentic voice, self-advocacy, and making connections. It's also a hero's journey; one in which each reader can participate.

The Art of Autism has become an international movement bringing together like-minds, self-advocates, parents, professionals, and organizations collaborating to shift and awaken possibilities for our talented populace with special needs. This book, and the previous book, is already giving center stage for its artists to shine brightly, to create inspired futures, and to provide those who participate, powerful and poignant stories of the human spirit in all its wisdom.

For some of the artists, this book may be a first step. It's up to the individual artist to use the book to open opportunities in their own communities and beyond. Four of the artists have made the leap into the international community. Seth Chwast, Ryan Smoluk, J.A. Tan and Trent Altman have been selected for 2012 United Nations World Autism Day stamps. You can see their work in the pages that follow.

The spirits and stories of seventy-five artists and poets from around the world are captured in this book. With all the differences and nuances of autism, from one individual to another, a common thread exists: the multi-faceted works of creative genius, self-expression, and communication beyond words.

The Art of Autism is your story too, because we know that within all of us is an artistic soul awaiting to emerge. You may not paint, but you may love music. If not music, perhaps you and your child can sway and rock to the movement of dance. You might be in tune with computers, building things (or taking them apart) or know how to make people laugh. You may twirl to a prism of color in the sunlight.

The arts and their creative expression encourage the development of skills and complement other therapies. When cultivated, the arts can expand one's horizons into adulthood, when tremendous growth holds the potential to explode beyond one's wildest imagination.

Please join us in *The Art of Autism* experience. If you'd like more information about how you can be a part of the art, contact us through www.the-art-of-autism.com.

Keri Bowers is the founder of *Normal Films Productions*. She is an international speaker, film producer, and author. Her website is www.normalfilms.com.

SELF-REFLECTIONS

Luna TMG *Window Reflection Paris*

"The rainbow mirrors human aims and action. Think, and more clearly wilt thou grasp it, seeing life is but light in many-hued reflection." Goethe

BEATRICE LEPROUST (aka Luna TMG, Luna The Moon Girl, 1972, Dijon, France)

Beatrice, whose professional name is Luna TMG, is a self-taught photographer, has exhibited her work in France and in the United States. Luna has several fascinations which dominate her thoughts and art. These include reflections, cats, and vegan cooking. All of Luna's photographs are actual scenes she has found - they are not montages. *"I see the world through little details. I must add each of these details, one after another, to have a general view of things."* Luna's work can be viewed at www.flickr.com/photos/lunatmg.

Everywhere & Nowhere   2009   Photograph

"*Most of the time in my pictures I'm trying to combine two universes in one, like an attempt to create a kind of bridge between two worlds. That's why I'm fascinated by reflections; I feel like 'Alice Through the Looking Glass.' The object isn't as important as the reflections.*"

Luna TMG 2010 *The Whole World in a Bottle* Photograph

The Whole World in a Bottle is important to Luna because as she says, "*It represents what I'm living. Do you know what it's like living in a painful glass ball? Behind a window all the time, being aware of this invisible wall, … even when you are surrounded by other people or your own family?*"

From Standifer Scott, *Autistic Fixation Shapes Photographer's Unique Images* (2011)

JACK CARL ANDERSON (1959, Bellingham, Washington)
In the past, Jack isolated himself from people for long periods of time. He received his diagnosis of Asperger's Syndrome in 2011. Now with the help of his partner, Mike, he's able to discover healthy ways to acknowledge and handle the behavioral aspects of his diagnosis. In 2011, Jack and Mike created *HeART of the Spectrum Autistic Community Center* which focuses on allowing individuals on the spectrum to explore their creative talents in an autism friendly environment. See Jack's art at theartofthespectrum.com/jack-carl-anderson

Silver Birch in Sunlight   2010   24 x 34"   Acrylic on canvas

"Because each day I feel so deluged with input, words, and distractions, I keep my creative style simple, graphic, and conceptually direct. At the age of 52, with my art, I have discovered a creativity that brings out in me a new-found discipline, focus, and ability to find the extraordinary in the ordinary. Although I feel pretty detached from the humanity around me, I find mental and spiritual freedom in the natural world: trees, water, open spaces, and the sky. As I examine this past year of my art, our new autistic art gallery, and my diagnosis, I must say, isn't self-discovery grand?!"

Jack Carl Anderson *Summoned to Hades* 2010 20 x 15"
Acrylic paint and metallic pewter glaze on canvas

Summoned to Hades depicts a sense of the forces in the world outside our control.

FRANK ALLEN (1980, Bedfordshire, England)
Frank is employed as a qualified play worker (a common term in England). He has a degenerative eye condition called Retinitis Pigmentosa which will eventually render him blind. Frank has always created art and music in a sporadic manner and is constantly surprised by the tunes and artworks the subconscious can conjure up. Frank has drawn comics and studied graphic design, yet finds it creates far too much anxiety to work in that environment. See his daily art at www.frankart.co.uk. *"Many people's art and music is restricted by too many rules and restrictions, stifling their creativity. More interesting art would be around if people were encouraged to follow their instincts instead of what they feel is expected."*

Asperger's Mind 2011 5.9 x 42 cm. Markers on paper

"When I finally received the diagnosis, I felt blessed and relieved. The diagnosis meant I'm not crazy or psychotic - nor am I alone. Knowing why I have troubles and awkwardness in certain situations doesn't always help others to understand me, but ultimately is an issue with them, and no longer has the power to bring me down. I would've felt in the dark with the diagnosis if I hadn't found Asperger's so interesting. Receiving the diagnosis has been a liberating experience and has given me confidence."

Frank Allen *Astro Light* 2011 42 x 5.9 cm. Markers on paper

"*Certain members of my family still think Asperger's is some notion I have in my head, because they don't want to accept the symptoms as being strange in themselves.*"

STEVEN SELPAL (1950, Palm Bay, Florida)
Steven, who was misdiagnosed with schizophrenia and other mental disorders for most of his adult life, was relieved to receive an Asperger's diagnosis. Steven has recently been chosen for Temple Grandin's book *Different, Not Less* about people successfully living on the spectrum. *"My drawing skill developed from a desire to reach a common ground of understanding with people. Watching people speak with the ease of just a few words combined with innuendo and body language has always been a mystery to me."*

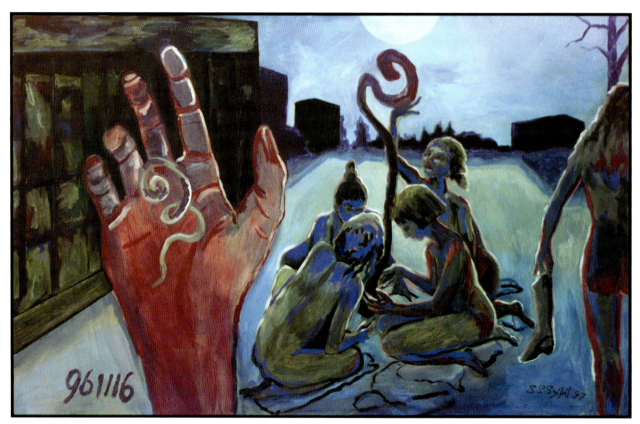

Dim of January Moon 1997 45 x 72" Acrylic on canvas

"My life inside my mind has always been enriched with a constant flood of mental images, which mostly proved to be a detriment unless I could apply my concentration to some form of art. Art is really a survival mechanism to me. All my life I earned my living by doing art of some kind, which included graphic design, illustration and painting. However, my first formal art training was in sculpture. Recently, I am merging the skills of sculpting and painting in my latest work and I am very excited about that."

Steven Selpal
Temple Grandin bas relief, 2011
28 x 18 x 3"
Fiberglass images
Multiples sculpture

These two bas reliefs were created by Steven in 2011 as part of a series of historical renditions of people who have influenced autism history.

Steven Selpal   *Stephen Shore*   2011   Diptych painted bas relief
Each panel 48 x 59 x 2.25" Acrylic on wood panel, sculpt and cast cement

"When people look me in the eye, I feel molecules sucking out of me, my energies diminishing. At the same time, I would forget what I am saying. Since February 1968, this symptom diminished a great deal, but it did not go away completely."

KIMBERLY GERRY-TUCKER (1964, Seymour, Connecticut)
Kim is an artist, poet, and published author. Her art work *Shattered Mirror* was featured on the cover of *Artism: The Art of Autism*, by Debra Hosseini. Kim has written a book about her life titled *Under the Banana Moon: A True Story of Living, Loving, Loss and Asperger's* (2011). "Art is a cathartic outlet for my frustration at not 'measuring up.' Thank goodness I can express myself through my art."

Whirling Dervishes, 2011
8 x 12"
Acrylic on paper

"As a kid I collected pencil shavings, sparkly things from gutters, and rocks. I sat on boulders in the woods for hours staring at lights through the tree canopy above. I avoided other kids. I had a huge vocabulary, yet when I spoke I was different. I didn't know others like me existed until I was diagnosed at age thirty-five. That was a revelation. A reason. An explanation. A happy day!

"At age forty-seven, I reflect on how things were, how things are, and where they're going. What would I be like today without the love and support of loving parents? I'm fairly certain I wouldn't function as well as I do. Though I've retained a whimsical, childlike manner, I'm a guarded person, and in many ways socially isolated. I'm as complex as I am simple. I see myself as strong, funny, and tough as nails. I'm an animal lover, who is quiet but sometimes screams on the inside.

"I know facts about amazing things - such as where Einstein vacationed with his wife, and what Van Gogh wrote in letters to his brother, yet there are times I don't understand simple words. This is hard to explain, but is serious to me. I hate being frustrated or confused. My mind twirls objects around in images that look like unidentifiable Picasso shapes. I can hear words like "tuna fish" and completely forget what those words mean.

"With my sensitivities I may run from a flushing toilet, if I'm stressed. I try to focus on my abilities. I turned my love of research into part-time legal research, and am studying to be a veterinary assistant. I turned my love of writing into freelance work.

"My life is about the journey, and I don't regret any of the sparklies I've picked up along the way. Not one!"

STILL LIFE

old-world

still life

time-eroded

faded brick

hint of a mansion

never built

old packhorse

dark wet sand

wind and rain

matte black line

moving into the background

end of the trail

entering another world

kinetic individual

lifelike laughter

of the faeries

up on the dark peak

natural rock formations

miscellany of the fascinating

withdrawn

from the tumult of the world

"go-it-alone"

take drama to new heights

in broken splendour

shameless coastal castle

still life

Kimberly Gerry-Tucker *Dusky Trees* 2011 8 x 12" Acrylic on canvas

FELLOW ASPIES

I call upon you, my fellow aspies,
to awake, and enlighten the human world
to the long-buried truth of Asperger's Syndrome
so that people can learn some new angles on life,
including the doctrines of substance over style.
As you sit in the dark womb
of a flickering planetarium,
call your true self into being.
Let the Orion constellation guide you
on the search through a wilderness
where you dodge ironclad bigots
and solve the hieroglyphics
of everyday communication.
Stay on the search
and you will find those who appreciate
the Aspergian magic you weave
when you take them on a cruise
in the life-like waters of a 3-D picture,
or cut Christmas cookie dough into Kwanzaa shapes,
or re-invent the automobile
to free us from the expensive tyranny of petroleum.
But whatever you do, be assured
that Aspergian tutelage will guide you
into the rebirth of day.

CHRISTOPHER WOOD-ROBBINS (1965, Stow, Massachusetts)
Chris often volunteers for such causes as Black History Month events and fundraising walks to support battered women's shelters. He also writes poems to praise the virtues of individuality, equality and autism awareness. He lives with his sweetheart, Julie Simoes.

DR. MICHAEL MCMANMON (1949, Lee, Massachusetts)
Dr. McManmon started drawing trees as a small child and his fascination continues to this day. He is the father of six children (one adopted) and has eleven grandchildren. He is the founder of the College Internship Program (CIP) which serves students with learning differences in six locations in the United States. In 2001, his staff diagnosed him with an autism spectrum disorder and he was later formally diagnosed with Asperger's. He works in pen and ink, watercolor, and oil. Dr. McManmon has written a book about his life called *Made For Good Purpose* (Jessica Kingsley, 2012).

Michael McManmon *Canopy* 2008 10 x 14" Watercolor

"I feel like I am the poster-boy for late diagnosis. It feels wonderful inside to know that all the 'goofy sides' of my personality are my best ones, and I can embrace them. I accept myself the way I am, knowing that I was made exactly the way I am, for good purpose under heaven. This is what I bring to the world now."

LISA ANTRAM (1964, Henderson, Nevada)
Lisa, who owns a successful online communications company, Catalina Communications, is also an accomplished and passionate portrait painter. Married for over twenty years, Lisa is the mother of two, the youngest of whom was born with autism. While obtaining a diagnosis for him, she realized she was on the spectrum as well, and subsequently received a diagnosis of Asperger's. The diagnosis changed her life so profoundly that she felt a dire need to help others. She has provided advocacy and expertise to support legislative and community initiatives which have helped the disability community in Nevada. Her websites are catalinacom.com and antramart.com.

Michelle   2011   20 x 16"   Oil on canvas

Lisa Antram *Girl with the Pearl Earring* 2011 20 x 16" Oil on canvas
In the likeness of the original by Vermeer

"Art is such a personal thing. I have trouble with being personal. So, being a realist seems appropriate for someone with Asperger's syndrome. I'm in awe of the other artists on the spectrum who are not realists. They manage to convey emotion in a way I'm not sure I ever could. Perhaps that is why I prefer portrait work. I can borrow the sitter's emotion and place it in the canvas to be reflected back at the viewer. I guess that is what my art means to me: being able to capture someone else's moment and share it with others. It is personal for them. It makes them and their loved ones happy while allowing me to remain outside of it."

AMANDA LAMUNYON (1995, Enid, Oklahoma)
Amanda began reading at age four. Teachers first noticed her artistic ability in Kindergarten when she drew all her ABC's instead of cutting out pictures for them. She began painting at seven years of age. She was diagnosed with Asperger's syndrome at the age of eight. Amanda was happy as a child, but lost confidence when she couldn't fit in at school. Her art changed everything. She began to express herself through painting, impressing her peers. She has garnered many awards for her art and gives back to charities. In 2011, she won a "Kohl's Kids Who Care" scholarship. Amanda shares her story with all who will listen. Her website is www.amandalamunyon.com.

Amanda painted *Sunflowers* at the age of seven.

Sunflowers, 2002
11 x 14"
Acrylic on canvas

"My art is very personal. I feel like part of me is coming out of my hands."

A LITTLE SECRET

Amanda LaMunyon (2006) age 11

She looks like any other girl.
But she has a secret
You may never suspect.

Lots of things bother her.
In her clothes, a little tag might feel like sand paper.
Food needs to taste just right
Or she won't eat it.
She thinks she can't go a week without ice cream.

Noise and movement are confusing.
It makes her want to run or say be quiet.
Light is a hundred times brighter to her.
Oh, what a world she lives in.

Some say she is a 'little professor.'
But you might not be interested in what she has to say.
She might start talking about Ancient Egypt or something else
And you won't have a clue what she is talking about.

She would never hurt anyone's feelings
But sometimes she does and she doesn't even know it.

What is this little secret?
Asperger's syndrome,
A high functioning form of autism.
I know because I have it.

Many are suspected of having it, Einstein, Michelangelo.
1 out of every 110 children will be diagnosed with autism this year.

Some say it is a disability.
But, I am a girl with dreams.
I will take what God has given me
Along with the challenge and use it
To fulfill the purpose God has for me.

Psalms 139: 13 & 14 says:
For you created my inmost being: you knit me together in my mother's womb.
I praise you because I am fearfully and wonderfully made.
Your works are wonderful,
I know that full well.

I give this challenge to you: If you know someone a little
Different, look for something good; it will be there.
For it may be a little secret waiting to be told,
A dream waiting to unfold.

NATALIE TOTIRE (1972, Chicago, Illinois)

As a child Natalie only drew flowers. Later she would include animals in her drawings. Not until many years later, did she start feeling comfortable drawing people. *"My art isn't just a hobby or a career. I have to use it to think and remember. If I don't draw it or write something down, I barely remember it or my mind wanders away. I have to catch my straying thoughts each time with my right hand and start drawing a picture or work on a craft."*

Cat in Space   2005   11 x 14"   Oil

Safe-T Puppet
Natalie has created a line of puppets.
This one is created for children with
autism because the eyes are sewn in.

"If Asperger's Syndrome were albinoism, I would probably look like a piebald, the other half with ADD. That's what I've learned knowing myself through the years and my family history, but not all diagnoses are easy to pinpoint. Mix it together and you get a jack of all trades in a certain area, like a tree with multiple branches. Mine is mostly in visual art. Bouncing from graphic design and fine arts to getting a degree in education at Moody Bible Institute, I learned to put it together and found that becoming a childrens' book writer and illustrator has become my goal. I've also used my talent to invent various puppets and use them in Sunday School. I have found that using puppets has really helped me connect more with the children I work with. I get lots more smiles, and can allow my puppet to act dumb and get away with it."

ACCEPTANCE

Are you liked?
probably.
How many friends do
you have?
And how many people do
you know?
lots, I'd say.
Do you gossip?
do you tease or maybe
expect everyone to be
the same?
answer yes to these
then you must be
neurotypical.
What about me?
I do none of these
things.
I'm different,
quirky
smart.
I say what I mean
and I mean what I say.
If I tease I do not
mean to
and gossip is not
my thing.
I do not expect
everyone to be
the same
like you do.
when I flap my hands
and rock
back and
forth
It means I'm having
a great time
Don't get mad if
I don't understand.

ISABELL DOUCETTE (1996, Vancouver, Canada)
"I am...Isabell. I like books, Justin Bieber, shoes. I like to read and eat lots of chocolate. Honesty, humor, and kindness are important to me. I like to laugh at my own jokes, even if they're not funny. But hate taking instructions from my peers. I don't like to hurt other people's feelings. And hate Monday mornings. But love to read for hours on end. The weekends and Tuesday are the best." Isabell's favorite quote is by Ralph Waldo Emerson: *"To be yourself in a world constantly trying to make you something else is the greatest accomplishment."*
isabelldoucette.yolasite.com *A Different Point of View*

GERHARD BECK (1951, Palatinate, Germany)
Gerhard studied Political Science, English, Law, and Social Pedagogics. He worked as a taxi driver in Berlin for sixteen years. Now he lives in the North of Germany with his girlfriend Birgit, five dogs and six cats. In 1999, after reading a book on Asperger's he suspected that he may be affected. His self-diagnosis was confirmed that same year by a psychiatrist. Gerhard's wax pastels and pencil drawings have been displayed in exhibitions in Essen and Berlin.

ASPERGER

Earliest childhood

What is lacking? The doctors would like to know.

Delays, limitations

Lack of practical experience and common sense

Don't look at me that way, so stiffly

Where is the abundance of meaning?

Too close to other persons

And this way of speaking, so precocious

And this endless pausing

Woefully little mutuality

Where is empathy?

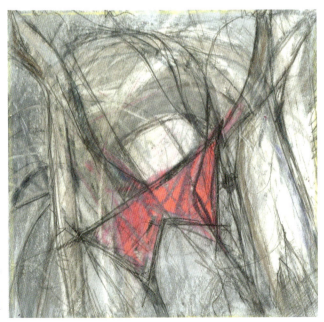

Untitled, 1996
11.8 x 12.2 cm.
Wax pastels and pencil

THE JOURNEY

Ryan Smoluk *The Path* Selected for 2012 United Nations stamp for World Autism Day

"The journey between what you once were and who you are now becoming is where the dance of life really takes place."   Barbara DeAngelis

Myths, Autism and the Artist
Darold A. Treffert, M.D.

"Why does he draw and produce? It is his life. It is his spirit."
    Takashi Kawasaki (Teacher): on Japan's savant artist Yoshihiko Yamamato

It is unclear exactly when the first art by a person with autism appeared. Some say it dates back to earliest times. Whenever it first happened, the world ever since has been brightened by the work of these unique individuals who possess such remarkable talent. This book is vivid testimony to their extraordinary abilities. Their art is a gift to us.

There are some particular things to remember about these artists and their work.

First, art by persons with autism stands on its own. Many artists with autism demonstrate superior skills by any standard. Their art work is spectacular and pleasing not just because it was created by someone with a disability, but it is spectacular and pleasing in its own right. Its merits astound. Look at the drawings and paintings in this book. To term this "outsider art," as the unenlightened may do, is elitist, demeaning and discriminatory. While certain of these artists lack formal training, they are most certainly capable of creating "insider art;" their lack of formal training may actually be part of what makes their work spectacular.

Second, in my view and in the opinion of many others as well, the remarkable abilities of the artist with autism surface because of their autism, not in spite of it. Many of their unique abilities co-exist along side certain of their "dis-abilities." In short, these skills are not merely compensatory, nor are they the product of continual reinforcement. Rather, they are integral to the "disorder," consistent with the spectrum's unusual sensitivity to various sensory stimuli, superior visual memory, precocious performance impulses and innate access to what has been called a "picture lexicon" or the "rules of art."

Third, these skills are not accidental, extraneous or frivolous. They represent the language - sometimes the only language - by which these individuals are able to communicate. Their creations convey their impressions, thoughts and emotions, when typical language and expression is limited or, in some cases, all together absent. Just as important and critical, these abilities serve as what I call, *a conduit toward growth,* in which language acquisition, social comfort, and daily living skills, are all enhanced.

This artwork not only enhances our lives as its beneficiaries, but also enhances the lives of the artists themselves: *training the talent* helps ameliorate other limitations. For many years I have witnessed this marvelous transition in many of the artists with autism I have had the honor to follow. Know too that, with these overall gains in functioning, there is no *dreaded trade-off* of special abilities whatsoever. Rather, both the special skills, language, social, and daily living skills advance simultaneously. Rest assured, one need not fear the loss of special abilities as a result of paying attention to them, much less other developmental needs.

Fourth, another myth is that artists with autism, while demonstrating spectacular duplication and replication skills, lack creativity, is just that: a myth. Artists with autism can definitely be creative. Indeed, having had the opportunity to follow a number of these artists with autism over the years, I have observed a predictable and marvelous pathway to creativity in these special people. They begin their artistic careers with striking replicas of what they have seen and stored, usually requiring no model or constant reference piece. An initial glance is often sufficient, to foster creation of dazzling replications, replete with minute detail.

On occasion, some improvisation appears - a telephone pole deleted there, a new tree placed here - and the original replication begins to be transformed. Then, along the way, comes interpretation, free form style, or some other form of creativity expressed in fresh, original work.

Thus is the path from literal copying, to improvisation, to free form creation, traveled. Some artists prefer to stay with replication, but many go beyond copying, as stunning as that can be, to improvising and then creating something entirely new.

I have seen musicians who are autistic follow the same path. First they play back exactly what they have heard, immediately committing it to memory. Then they begin improvising. Finally, after a time, entirely original compositions emerge. Research studies comparing childhood musicians who are autistic with a control group of non-autistic musicians with some musical training, show "musical inventiveness" to be higher in the group with autism. When compared to neuro-typical control groups - even groups with training - based on my observations, I expect the finding of increased inventiveness to surface among artistic children with autism.

Another myth that begs discreditation, is that the art of persons with autism lacks emotion. This myth suggests that, while the works of artists with autism may demonstrate incredible skills in replicating, even unusual color or technique, the artwork is emotionally flat. Not so. Look at the works in this book. Even artists with autism who may lack the ability to show emotion in any other way, brightly and forcefully share their emotions through their art. For some of these artists their art presents a way for them to venture out emotionally for the first time. For those of us who are attentive, their art provides a link to better understanding and communicating with these remarkable individuals.

Finally, so importantly, behind each of these artists is a mom or dad, sister or brother, teacher, caretaker or other individual who has been integral to discovering, nurturing, encouraging and celebrating the abilities of these artists on the autism spectrum. Love is a good therapist too. Seeing a Dad celebrate—literally—his son's work, witnessing the "that's my girl" pride in a Mom's conversation about her daughter's work, is heartwarming and inspiring.

I have been interested in autism and special abilities as a doctor and a scientist. During my journey with these artists and their equally amazing families, teachers and friends, I have learned as much about "matters of the heart" and things of "human interest," as I have about disorders, synapses or circuits, and other topics of "scientific interest."

At the art exhibit in Wisconsin titled, "Windows of Genius: Artwork of the Prodigious Savant," hundreds visited-- townspeople from all walks of life, and students from kindergarten to graduate school. All marveled at the art, and were amazed at what each of the exhibit's artists could do. In the process of getting to know the artists better, through their art and discussions about them, appreciation steadily grew for who each artist is as a person. Along the way a clearer understanding of autism also evolved. Everyone gained from that event.

My hope for this book is the same. By seeing the art and learning about the artists, readers and society at large will focus less and less on autism and its "dis-abilities,"appreciating and celebrating more than ever, the unique abilities we all possess.

I don't know when the first artwork by a person with autism appeared. I do know that marvelous capacity continues and I appreciate that we, along with these remarkable artists, can walk a path together as its fortunate beneficiaries.

Darold A. Treffert, M.D. is the author of *Extraordinary People: Understanding Savant Syndrome* and *Islands of Genius*. His website is www.savantsyndrome.com.

QAZI FAZLI AZEEM (1981, Karachi, Pakistan)

Qazi is South Asia's first self-advocate for autism. He runs the non-profit www.autismpakistan.org which is the only website in Pakistan for giving free advice to parents, doctors, and special educators. Qazi is the main contributor to the *Pakistan Autism Meetup Group,* a free online advice and meeting forum for parents and special educators, serving people of Pakistani origin on the spectrum. He has led the autism awareness campaigns in Pakistan since 2008 for the United Nations World Autism Awareness Day. Qazi was honored with his recent inclusion in the book *"A History of Autism: Conversations with the Pioneers"* by Adam Feinstein (Wiley, UK, 2010).

The Painted Jackal   2011   8 x 10"   Digital media

The concept behind "The Painted Jackal" is based on a story written by Sufi scholar, Jalaluddin Rumi, about the masks people wear to fit in, be accepted and conform to society.

Self Portrait, 2009
20 x 16"
Digital media

THE PATH TO CELEBRATION

For those with lives worth celebrating,
To you these words are worth dedicating
To proudly smile when you've been blessed
With talent, progress, and success.
And the effort used to overcome
Old obstacles that made you glum
You're much more now than you were then
You prove it time and time again.

The start was the hardest part because
You were shown the dark for what it was.
You learn to cope, and slowly you give
All you have to defiantly live
Against any odds, doubts, or distractions.
They pale in comparison to your actions.
You've built yourself a solid foundation.
A milestone worth it's own celebration.

Adversity dares us to be more,
To step up to the plate,
Whether strike or sore
To state our challenges right in the eye
And swing even if we risk a pop fly.
We're reminded not to keep ourselves in the dark
When those in common shoes knock one out of the park
Stoking our own sense of validation,
A kind of inspiration worth celebration.

When you unlock unseen potential
The growth that emerges is exponential.
Step back. Reflect! You'll be surprised
When the seeds you sow are realized.
You'll see those around you have a sense
Of your well evolved self-confidence.
And life just can't help but congratulate
The winner in you...
And that's why we celebrate!

JAMES S. RAPHAEL (1976, Goleta, California)
James has been writing poetry, lyrics, and keeping personal journals since he was ten. James enjoys singing and playing guitar and bass. He's fascinated by electrical towers which he enjoys taking photos of, as well as building models of them out of Tinker Toys. Roadways also fascinate James - especially elaborate freeway interchanges. James lives independently.
"Writing and other practices of self-expression are crucial to my well-being, especially coming from a background of communication challenges."

ESTHER BROKAW (1960, Preston, Connecticut)
Esther is an untrained artist, who over the last twenty years, has created a collection of acrylic, watercolor, and oil paintings. Each painting exhibits an unusual focus to color and detail. Recently, Esther came forward to speak publicly about her diagnosis and art. Esther has had a number of careers in her life, including waitress, carpenter and roofer. At the age of thirty, she had enough time and resources to dedicate her time to painting and raising her children. Esther is classified as a savant. She's able to see complex patterns most people can't. Esther was the Autistically Natural (ANCA) award winner for 2011. Her daughter Isabel is featured in this book as well. More of Esther's work can be seen at www.savantgallery.

Nude   1991   20 x 30"   Oil on belgian linen

"I didn't have the confidence or funds to hire a model; I used a picture of myself. I played with the colors of blues in the shadows. I wove pinks and golds and other colors into the flesh tones."

Esther Brokaw   *Autumn on Fire*   18 x 24"   Oil on belgian linen

Esther's art continuously unfolds into beautiful, expressionistic oil paintings of scenes, people, and sights that inspire her. She paints from photos she has taken herself, adding her own touch and light to the scene surprising even herself with what ends up on the canvas. Though Esther continues to recover from celiac disease and mercury poisoning, she lives happily in Connecticut with her husband, Andrew, two children and four dogs.

SETH CHWAST (1983, Cleveland Heights, Ohio)
At age eighteen, Seth was evaluated for a career in dry mopping. He took his first art class at twenty, was featured on the *Today Show* as an artist at twenty-three, and was invited back at twenty-four. Before Seth turned twenty-eight, he had international exhibitions in the Galapagos Islands and the National Gallery of the Cayman Islands. In America, Seth has had exhibitions at Dartmouth, the Cleveland Clinic and twice at the Cleveland Museum of Natural History. In 2011, he participated in a "Neurodiversity" exhibit at the Museum of Modern Art of the Ukraine and he had a successful exhibit in Curaçao. Seth provided the cover art for three medical textbooks and was featured in two documentaries. Seth's website is www.sethchwastart.com. To Seth, famous means *"Make people happy. Grow your brain. New friends are everywhere."*

Self Study in Blue/Green
2005
62 x 52"
Acrylic on canvas

"What if [Seth] is oriented to altitude, longitude, latitude, temperature, and humidity in ways that we are not? Seth's auditory ability is amazing. He can name any chord or any four random notes struck together for an instant on a piano…

"Does he see differently? What if he takes in what we lack the sensitivity to pick up, and what if he lacks the ability to filter out what we reflexively ignore? He may have abilities that are not yet recognized or understood, let alone acknowledged or admired. He may have gifts and problems we miss because of our assumptions of what we all can do."

Debra Chwast, *An Unexpected Lfe* (Sterling Publishing, 2011)

Seth Chwast *Mythic Creatures Mural* (3 of 7 panels) 2011 36 x 78" Acrylic on canvas
The first panel was selected for a United Nations stamp for World Autism Day 2012

Seth Chwast
Fantasy Hippocampus #1, 2008
36 x 48"
Oil on canvas

Seth *"is an icon of hope. He brings joy. His story is the way 'Never give up' walks the earth."*
  Debra Chwast, *An Unexpected Life* (2011)

YOM TOV BLUMENTHAL (1974, Sfat, Israel)

Yom Tov graduated from the Ringling School of Art and Design in Sarasota, Florida in 1998. In 2010, after embracing his Jewish identity he moved to Sfat, Israel, better known as the "Artist Corner" or "City of the Mystics." Yom Tov shows his work in many galleries in the United States. Ben Goldman, a film producer who produced a video about Yom Tov, has referred to Yom Tov's art as "Modern art in an Ancient City." Quotes below and on the next page are from Yom Tov's website yomtov.com.

Shalom from Zefat   2011   50 x 70 cm.   Acrylic on canvas

"Some people would say I had 35 years of 'bad days.' At 35, I decided to start my life over and move to Israel. On that day, about January 1, 2010, I asked my father if he knew my Hebrew name. He didn't remember it but he said, 'I may have your Bris Milla certificate in my closet.' He found my certificate and it said 'Your name is Yom Tov!'... So, after 35 years of a somewhat out of control psychological nightmare, I find out my name is "Good Day." How ironic!

..."I finally feel that I am on a solid path to becoming the person I have always dreamed of becoming and G-d willing, I can help others who have a different and unique way of seeing the world..."

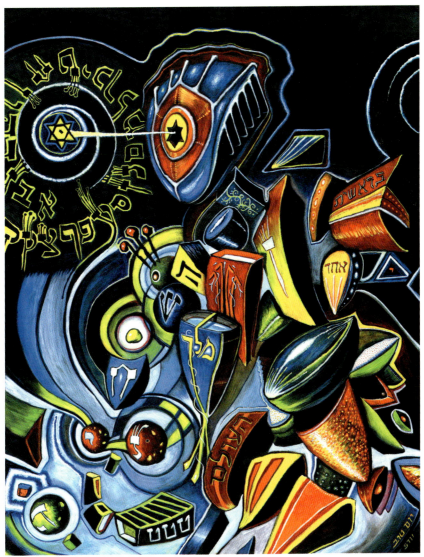

Yom Tov *Quad Spiral* 2011 70 x 50 cm. Oil on canvas

"I was just a small child in the bank with my mother. I was running around the bank practically jumping off the walls. A woman came up to my mother and said, 'Is his name Michael?' My mother was quite surprised and responded with, 'Yes, how do you know?' The woman said, 'You should have never named him Michael. All Michael's are like this.' ...

"When I was a child we were in McDonalds with my aunt. My mother asked me if she could have a sip of my milk shake. So I threw it in her face! Why I did this, I do not know, and I do not remember doing it. I think I was just too creative for my own brain.

"We were all over my aunt's house one day. I ran into the kitchen where everyone was hanging out, with a big smile across my face, saying, 'Come look it is snowing in the living room!' When they came into the living room, they saw that I had dumped powdered laundry detergent all over the furniture, and all over everything! This too I don't remember doing...

"Life is weird! I am not sure what G-d was thinking when he made my brain way too creative for my body! Supposably I have a watered down case of autism called Ass-Burgers (with a side of fries and a milk shake). But who knows! I have been diagnosed for every possible brain disorder on the planet by several different professionals across the globe, and was given almost every different type of brain medication to suppress it all."

ROHAN SONALKAR (1971-2007, Pune, India)
After a robust and healthy childhood in the Himalayan village of Tezpur, Rohan entered an urban school and slowly regressed into a recluse. His epileptic episodes were unrelenting. He was misunderstood by peers and ridiculed by teachers. After the sixth grade, he was denied education for want of a special school. He was eighteen before he received a diagnosis of autism. Art not only became an outlet for his creativity, but became his vocation. His art was highly praised in the U.S. and India during his life. Rohan passed away in 2007 after a sudden stroke, leaving behind a legacy of vibrant paintings. His work can be seen at www.sonalkar-art.com. *"My eyeballs are like the headlights of a car."*

Cyclists   1998   36 x 36"   Acrylic on canvas

Art became an outlet for Rohan's energies and, through it, he rebuilt his bruised identity and generated savings for the future. Rohan garnered international acclaim for his art, and through it all, he remained his natural autistic self, unmoved by compliments, courteous and content, yet with a poor concept of math and money. His artistic discipline and yoga were his hallmarks.

Rohan Sonalkar
Flutist, 2000
30 x 24"
Acrylic on canvas

Dolphins, 2004
24 x 30"
Acrylic on canvas

NERI AVRAHAM (1990, Newton, Massachusetts)

Neri expressed his emotions through his art at a young age. He began to paint with watercolors at age five. The family struggled with the lack of acceptance towards him and were concerned that he wasn't being seen beyond his autism. When he was eleven, the family immigrated to the United States from Israel in search of a better life for Neri. The numerous trips Neri took in his childhood influenced him and his art. Neri takes pride in his work and wants to expand the mediums he uses. He attends the Massachusetts College of Art. His aspiration is to be *"the best artist I can be."*

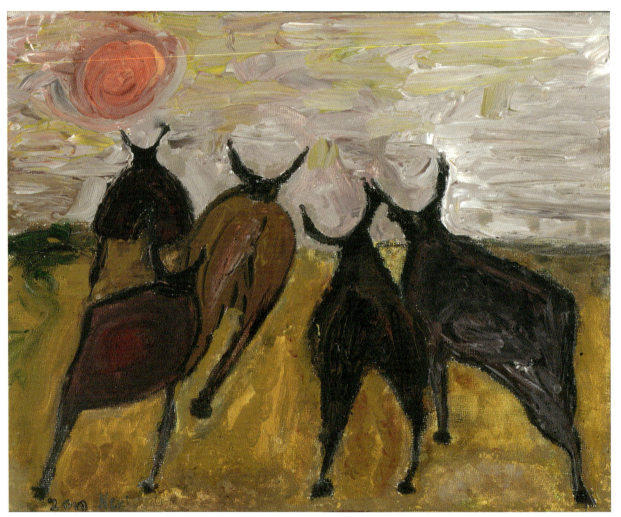

Escape   2010   8 x 10"   Acrylic

"I usually begin a new painting with random brush strokes of colors, then respond to the rhythm of the music and the direction the painting leads me; exploring a variety of methods of applying acrylic color on raw canvas and looking for new combinations I've never done before. My interest is to play with the colors and see what would happen if … At other times it appears that the painting already knows what it wants and I listen, watch … Painting allows me to become more comfortable with uncertainty and unpredictability. Painting spontaneously has been beneficial; it encourages my mind to be quiet and it helps me to have no concern for the approval of others."

ODE TO BIG BROTHER

Oh you big brother who is always here for me
Oh you big brother with a strong voice
That brings comfort to me
Oh you with a clear voice and a sharp sight
Oh, you brother that helps me
Everything around clear to see

Oh you big brother who can see through me
Capture best moments just for our shared memories
Oh you big brother best friend one can have
Oh you big brother forever and ever faithful you stay.

Neri Avraham   *Back Home*   2011   16 x 20" Acrylic

A special bond exists between Neri and his older brother, Orri. From a young age Neri would draw pictures of Orri and Orri would participate in Neri's therapies. If Neri got something, he would make sure Orri got something too. Nirith, Neri's mom says *"The acceptance and the commitment of the team who worked with us were the key to Neri's growth. Autism allows you to appreciate the child steps and because everything is in slow motion, you learn to appreciate the simple things - the everyday steps in learning, the beauty in nature, a kind word ... a nice smile."*

RYAN SMOLUK (1978, Winnipeg, Manitoba)

Ryan is an award winning Canadian artist who creates works of art in many mediums, including oils, acrylic, illustrative art, pottery and clay sculptures. Ryan is a powerful self-advocate and seasoned spokesperson for autism awareness. Nominated by Toyota Canada for the "Never Quit Award," Ryan is currently completing a bachelor degree in fine arts at the University of Manitoba. Ryan received international recognition by having his art work "The Path" selected by the United Nations for an Autism Awareness stamp in 2012. Ryan's work can be viewed at www.ryansmoluk.ca. *"Art stands on its own merit, it has no boundaries, it has no label."*

Embracing Change 2010 20 x 16" Acrylic

"I like to make a difference in the world - not all things in life are about making money. I want to inspire and give hope where I can. One day, I'd like to own my own home and find permanent work in the arts field.

"In the end, autism does not define us."

"When I was eleven years old, I had my first solo art show. It was my first touch of success. I had about thirty black and white drawings and paintings and about 16 clay sculptures. On opening night a radio station, local newspaper and some city council members came. It was all very exciting for me. For about two years just prior to turning twelve, I would only wear black and white clothing - and it couldn't have any logos or writing on it either. This was my black and white period where I only painted in black and white, and I saw life in only black and white. One day an artist asked me 'Why do you only use black and white?' I hadn't noticed! He suggested I introduce another color. I chose sky blue. Blue makes me calm."

PATTERNS

Sweet Sanibel Shore by Trent Altman

"To understand is to perceive patterns."
Isaiah Berlin

The Importance of Art and Music
Stephen Shore, Ed.D.

"Vibrant waves of sequenced patterns emerged in my head whenever I looked at musical notes and scores. Like pieces of a mysterious puzzle solved, it was natural for me to see music and its many facets as pictures in my head. It never occurred to me that others couldn't see what I saw."

When I was a child, music, laughter, and a conscious focus on my abilities filled our home. The radio, always tuned to classical or popular music stations, encouraged singing, movement, and playful narration. My parents, who were quite progressive for the times, defied the conventional wisdom of the mid-1960's; that I be institutionalized. Instead, they were determined to provide me with a foundation that emphasized music, creativity, movement, sensory integration, narration, and imitation. In today's terms, we would call their efforts an intensive home-based early intervention program, probably most closely related to the cognitive-developmental systems approach called the Miller Method.

My parents saw me as having an extremely diverse skill set with great potential to emerge my odd, if not quirky behaviors. They reasoned that in emphasizing my strengths, they could reach me in my isolation through creativity and intention. Their focus on awakening my spirit and abilities is what I suspect drives me to teach music to children with autism today. I believe my connection to music mirrors why many of us are involved in the arts: to give those on the autism spectrum, as well as persons viewing or enjoying their art, a greater appreciation for what it is to be human.

Today, in addition to traveling the world and sharing my methods, I teach at the university level, write books and articles on autism, and give music lessons solely to people on the autism spectrum. I consider myself a music educator, not a trained music therapist, yet my work helps achieve several therapeutic results, including improved motor control, communication, and social interactions. In giving a person on the autism spectrum a solid key through the arts, they are enabled in a relaxed environment to develop interactions with others. The learning of artistic theory and craftsmanship is always secondary to participating in the process, which develops self-esteem and an appreciation for others.

In recent years, an explosion of the popularity of the arts as interventions in autism is apparent. There is no doubt that parents and professionals who use the arts as specific and intentional tools are likely to achieve significant results in improved empathy, behaviors, and language. Music, in particular, provides an alternate means of communication for those who may be nonverbal, and for others it can assist in organizing verbal communication.

Whether it be music, drama, visual arts, comedy, dance, or other forms of the arts, I encourage parents to "play" in creativity with their kids. While not every child will respond to every form of the arts, within every child is a connection to one form or another and a potential waiting to be fulfilled. Find your child's artistic "carrot," and you'll open a door to possibilities beyond your wildest imaginations and dreams.

Dr. Stephen Shore presents and consults internationally on adult issues pertinent to education, relationships, employment, advocacy, and disclosure and is the author of *Beyond the Wall: Personal Experiences with Autism and Asperger Syndrome, Ask and Tell: Self-Advocacy, Disclosure for People on the Autism Spectrum, Understanding Autism for Dummies,* and the DVD *Living Along the Autism Spectrum: What it means to have Autism or Asperger Syndrome.*

CHARLES MEISSNER (1953, Silver Spring, Maryland)
Charles has a prodigious memory, an uncanny eye for geography, and a broad-ranging interest in people and the media. It was that combination which resulted in a invitation from NASA for Charles to create a work focused on the moon landing for the celebratory exhibit marking the 50th anniversary of space travel. Fans of Charles are drawn, in particular, to the stream of consciousness commentary that elucidates many of his pieces. Charles participates in the Art Enables program. *"I started drawing when I was two. I like drawing work, places ... anything."*

Off to Work   2011   11 x 19"   Watercolor on board

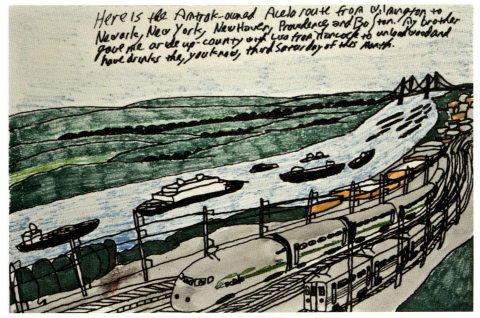
The Third Saturday   2011   19 x 25"   Watercolor and marker on paper

JESSICA PARK (1958, Williamstown, Massachusetts)
A nationally recognized self-taught artist with autism, Jessica is passionate about astronomy, Victorian architecture and urban skylines. Her detailed acrylic renderings of bridges, buildings, houses and churches have a distinctive and colorful pop art quality and otherworldly brilliance about them. In 2008, *Exploring Nirvana: The Art of Jessica Park*, a Massachusetts College of Liberal Arts book project was published documenting her dazzling artwork and remarkable life. Her website is www.jessicapark.com.

Flat Iron Building 2004   23.5 x 16.5" Acrylic on paper
Courtesy of Pure Vision Arts, New York

Jessica has 64 tubes of acrylic paint yet rarely uses the color of paint as it comes out of the tube. Each color is mixed to a particular shade and there will often be seven or eight shades of the same color which will be applied one by one according to a diagram that she holds in her mind from the beginning. (From Jessica Park's website)

Jessica Park *Chrysler Building with Periheleon and Transit of Venus #2* 2004
23 x 17" Acrylic on paper Courtesy of Pure Vision Arts, New York

NORA BLANSETT (1974, Nova Scotia, Canada)
Nora grew up as a world traveller, finding inspiration in the classic geometric patterns of the Middle East, India and Asia before moving to figurative and fantasy works. Her primary mediums are watercolor, pen and ink, as well as photography, jewelry and soft-sculpture dolls. She is a published author of poetry and short stories and finds profound joy in sharing her creations and thoughts. Nora was born in Alabama and resides in Canada with her husband. Her website is www.norablansett.com.

FINDING ME

I am an open window,
Through which I cannot see.
At one time it was clear,
and through it was me.
Now I am alone and lost,
I don't know where I stand.
My heart's in the clouds,
my feet forgotten on land.
I crawled out the window,
and searched everywhere --
but the land was barren,
my spirit wasn't there.
I took flight to scan,
searching the wild earth;
and eventually came to find
a secret glade and hearth.
In that place I considered
what I'd grown to be,
and in my search for self
I was simply finding me.

Sarah's Butterflies, 2011
7 x 5"
Watercolor and ink

Nora Blansett
Behind the Veil, 2011
7 x 5"
Watercolor and ink

"I had to come out of the 'autistic closet' because people often misinterpret my meaning or motives. Those who don't realize I'm autistic often assume that there is something 'wrong' with me and jump to incorrect conclusions. I can be childlike in some ways and often not taken very seriously, regardless of how desperately I'm trying to convey my thoughts or opinions. I'm extremely talkative, but my conversational skills are limited. I never known when it's my turn so I tend to talk and just go on and on. People get bored and walk away, or they tease me for my chattiness that just goes in circles and fails to be linear. There's a lot of confusion, so I get embarrassed and that just makes it worse."

PIPOYE (1997, Casablanca, Morroco)

Pipoye is a self-taught digital painter born in Casablanca. At age six he was diagnosed with autism. Two years later he made an amazing breakthrough when his parents gave him a computer. He discovered within the computer not only a best friend and teacher, but an entire world - the people, the languages, the cultures; all the amazing elements that constitute our universe. These discoveries have helped him become aware of what surrounds him and given him the ability to express himself. Pipoye is influenced by the artists Klimt, Kadinsky, Klee and Kahlo.

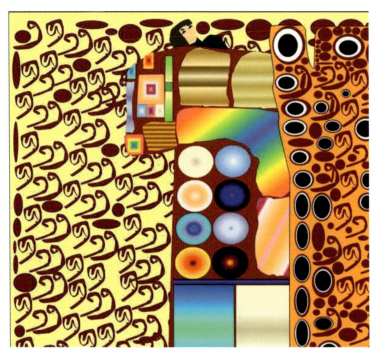

Klimtmania, 2011
Digital media

New York City 2011 Digital media

PIPOYE
Klimt2, 2011
Digital media

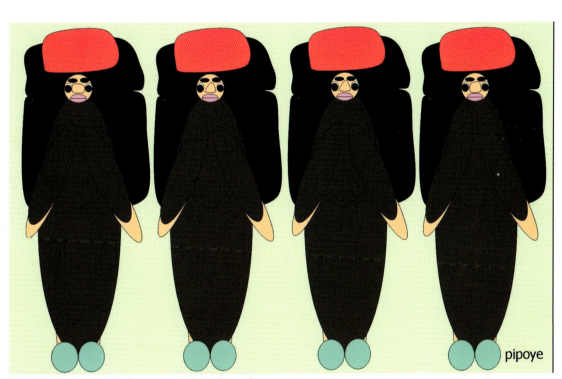

PIPOYE *Four Girls* 2011 Digital media

"Pipoye's artistic work is like traveling in a sweet, colorful, peaceful and beautiful world. His vision of life is full of optimism and joy. Cities and people are magical and delicious."
                                                                    Iman Chair, Pipoye's mom

SUSAN BROWN (1957, Sayville, New York)
Diagnosed with autism as a young child, Susan began drawing spirals, women and cars at the age of five. She was encouraged by her father, an engineer; her mother, a chemist; and her aunt, a sculptor. Brown first painted her characteristic grid-like drawings on cardboard in the 1980's while working as a dishwasher at Friendly's where cardboard packing was readily available. Her work reflects her eclectic interests in portraiture, transportation, and landscapes and is drawn from her prodigious memory of growing up on Long Island.

Her Mother, 2008
24 x 20"
Mixed media on cardboard

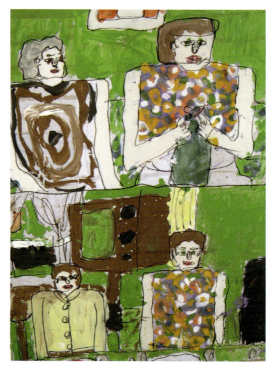

Family Portrait, 2006
24 x 20"
Mixed media on cardboard

Susan Brown *Mixed Grids* 2011 30 x 40" Mixed media on canvas

CRAIG ROVETA (1963, Brisbane, Australia)
Craig first explored expressing himself through color and movement of paint, on paper and canvas, at the Steiner school in Sydney during his teen years. This became his main form of communication and outlet for self expression, in an otherwise unvoiced life at that time. He has a natural and raw talent that is vivid, bold and evocative. In the last ten years, he has actively honed his natural talent and further explored his passion for vibrant colors.

Eden   2008   61 x 60 cm.   Acrylic on canvas

By sharing his art, Craig hopes others may benefit from many of the challenges he has faced and hopes to help create a more understanding and compassionate world where people are seen for all of who they are, not for what they can and cannot do.

Craig Roveta *Copper* 2007 35 x 43 cm.
Acrylic on canvas

THROUGH A DIFFERENT LENS

Craig Roveta

AUTISM is...

Hues of autumn brown

Flashes of angry red

And

Hopeless, cowardly yellow.

AUTISM is...

Seeing the world through a different lens

It is travelling in a car with a muddy

windscreen

The vehicle often breaks down

The driver cannot see clearly to reach his

destination

but

This vehicle is unique

It is mine

And it is how I am travelling

DANI BOWMAN (1995, La Canada, California)
Dani founded Powerlight Studios at age eleven, and has been working professionally since age fourteen, partnering with Joey Travolta, by teaching animation to others with autism at his summer camp program. She loves animation, illustration, and creating fun entertainment for children of all ages. Dani has a full slate of regular high school classes with a 3.8 GPA. Dani aspires to be the Temple Grandin of her generation, working to change the world's perception of autism and demonstrate all of the special abilities that people with autism have, while striving for acceptance and integration within society and employing others on the spectrum at Powerlight Studios. www.powerlight-studios.com.

The Adventures of Captain Yuron   2008   Digital media

"During 2008, as a seventh grader, after I was done with my classwork during history class, I asked my history teacher, Mr. Mispegal, to use some papers to make a book. While I was making a book, I thought about a hero being a fusion of many franchise characters such as Captain Underpants, Mametchi, Kizatchi, Billy Hatcher, 9-Volt from Nintendo, etc. Then suddenly, it revealed as a hero character named Captain Yuron, a creature with leafy ears, grassy hair attached to his green highlights on his head, pale blue skin, red cape and shoes, green eyes, white face and tummy."

Dani Bowman *Fleen* 2008 Digital media

Dani Bowman *Animatrobes* 2010 Digital media

J. MICHAEL VIDAL (1986, Arlington, Virginia)
Michael's love for art has helped him overcome many limitations of autism. At age two he isolated himself, lost language and eye contact, yet he started building Legos and drew on the walls. His mom homeschooled him from when he was seven until he graduated from high school in 2006. Michael is now enrolled in college pursuing a degree in graphic art. He aspires to be a cartoonist like his teacher and mentor former Disney artist, Albert Baruch. *"I may have autism, but autism does not have me."*

Skyline Paradise   2009   18 x 24"   Acrylic

"I feel blessed because I've learned a lot facing this challenge called autism; my son is the best gift in my life . . . God and the angels have helped me with my own diagnosis of Cerebral Palsy and my son's autism . . . My son changed my life completely and I like this change because I can help others."
Angelica Vidal, Michael's mom

Magnificent Monarch, 2011
18 x 24"
Acrylic

THE PROCESS

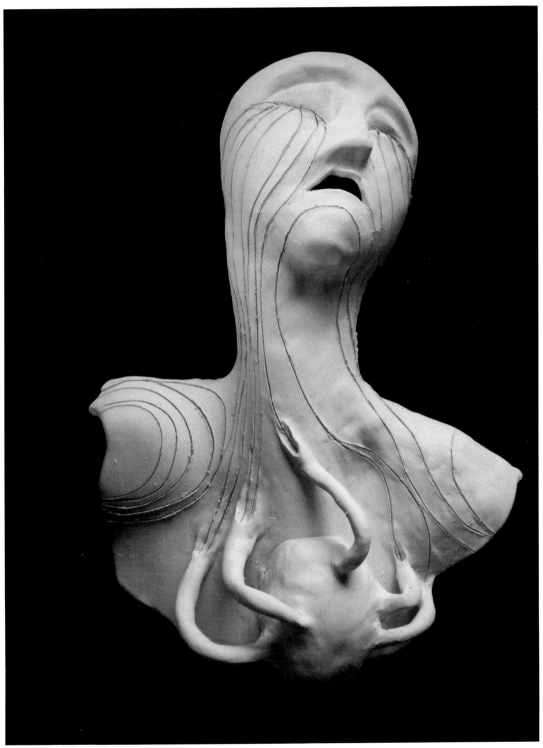

Kim Miller *The Agony*

"In every painting a whole is mysteriously enclosed, a whole life of tortures, doubts, of hours of enthusiasm and inspiration." Wassily Kadinsky

At Society's Growing Edge

Colin Zimbleman, Ph.D.

"Here the artist's relative lack of adaptation turns out to his advantage; it enables him to follow his own yearnings far from the beaten path, and to discover what it is that would meet the unconscious needs of his age."

C.G. Jung *

Autism is an exceptional phenomenon that has taken our cultural imagination by storm. It is exceptional because it continually eludes our definitions, expectations, and treatments, but also because it offers a chance for us to glimpse an awe-filled vision of the world that might otherwise pass us by.

If you have been touched by or attentive to the world of autism, then, chances are, you have noticed a certain high pitch or fervor regarding this subject. Mothers of children with autism battle pharmaceutical giants. Psychologists disagree as to whether to treat this disorder from a biological or a behavioral position, and self-advocates themselves question whether Autistic Spectrum Disorder should be considered a disorder at all rather than an alternative state of being in the world.

Having worked with children on the autism spectrum, I have witnessed many of these clashing perspectives. Yet, despite the public clamor surrounding this work, what stands out above all else are the autistic person's quiet, unexpected, and creative revelations. I have seen over and over again a capacity for profound expression that reveals an intimate and unimpeded relationship with their creative source. This takes any number of forms including writing, visual images, acting, and logic/critical reasoning – to name a few. One girl with autism, my charge in a third grade classroom, wrote this poem:

Stars are glittering
Like cosmic body glitter
So far away here on Earth
Yet so close. Flaming balls of gas.
We'll probably never find out
How they got there.
Sky tonight,
Black or inky, velvety, raven
With a dash of peacock blue

* (Essay entitled, "On the relation of analytical psychology to poetry" found in the book, *The Spirit in Man, Art, and Literature*. Published 1966 by Princeton University Press. Trans: R.F.C. Hull.)

It appears, as other people preoccupy themselves with conforming to socially accepted world views, people with autism remain steadfastly unique in their vision of the world, which, in turn, puts them in a key position to not only make beautiful poetic expressions, but also poignant observations of our individual and cultural assumptions and biases. Temple Grandin's work redesigning cattle slaughterhouses to make them more humane is a notable example of this.

There is another characteristic of autism that stands out and has been less widely recognized. Children with autism (and very likely adults with autism as well) seem to embody and magnify what is happening in the collective environment. I saw this while working in the third-grade classroom. The child who wrote the poem on the previous page seemed to function as an expressive conduit for what the class was experiencing but which for the most part was being contained just under the surface. In this way, persons with autism play much the same role in society, as do artists whose value lies in their ability to bring into consciousness what lies in the unconscious of the collective culture. This is why master artists have consistently challenged the status quo of their time. It is less a direct intention of the artist, but rather a by-product of their work.

Autism, too, is currently poised at the growing edge of our culture. It is a catalyst for change evidenced by the scale of the dialogue on this subject, the intensity of energy that revolves around it, and the extreme polarities of beliefs and positions taken. Artistic expression is most likely not the defining characteristic of autism. However, the fact so many of these individuals have uncanny gifts to express truths through creative work should not be overlooked. Their creativity and artwork is perhaps an appropriate metaphor for the role they play in society. Maybe it is not a coincidence the word "autistic" is so often confused with "artistic." Like a Freudian slip, there is more to it than first appears.

Colin Zimbleman received his doctorate in Clinical Psychology at Pacifica Graduate Institute in California. He is a graduate of Rhode Island Institute of Design and was Kevin Hosseini's first art mentor. He currently works as a therapist for STAR Autism Inc. in Ventura, California.

Autism ... offers a chance for us to glimpse
an awe-filled vision of the world that
might otherwise pass us by.

RICKY NESBITT (1971, Williamsville, New York)
Ricky who is deaf and autistic lives in a world without sound or words. At the age of 32, he began creating his unique form of art. His original pieces were small and were contained within circles the size of tea cups. As he progressed, he broke free of the circles and began to create works that stretched from eight feet to a whopping 220 feet in length. Now he photographs his collections of toys with a backdrop of color fields that he creates. Ricky resides in a group residence through Autistic Services, Inc. in New York.

Untitled   2008   30 x 40"   Photograph of mixed media

"Even though I knew Ricky was different growing up, he was always just my big brother. While we never had the 'normal' brother/sister relationship; it has been all I've ever known. I've always been fascinated by my brother - by just about everything he does - his unusual behaviors and the noises he makes, his obsession with animal figures, his beautiful and mysterious artwork. I've always wondered what goes on in his mind and still yearn to know. The relationship that my brother and I have is unique. It is something I cherish. My brother is my heart. His artwork allows us to enter a small part of his world and I am so happy that people have taken such an interest in it. I'm so very proud of my big brother."

Kristin Nesbitt, Ricky's sister

Ricky Nesbitt
Untitled, 2008
30 x 40"
Photograph of
mixed media

In this photograph, Ricky creates a world where man and beast cross paths in a surreal landscape.

Ricky Nesbitt
Untitled, 2008
30 x 40"
Photograph of
mixed media

Ricky places "*his personal collection of plastic animals on his color fields and photographs them, transforming his two-dimensional drawings into vibrant landscapes that envelop his toys and create a surrealistic backdrop for his serene and ambiguous wildlife narratives.*"

Autistic Services Art Works brochure for Ricky's one-man show

NEKEA BLAGOEV (1983, Mackay, Queensland, Australia)
Nekea, diagnosed with Asperger's, has created her own unique art form. By placing glass on top of canvas, she creates puzzled-like pictures best viewed by torch light in the darkness where they glisten with reflection creating their 3D effect. Nekea is talented in drawing, sculpture, printmaking, mixed media, photography, creative writing, painting and cooking signature meals. She is a radio show host on ANCA radio. Her website is getsmashedart.com.
"In my world art is an uncontrollable infection that must be delivered. I've always had a burning desire to be creative. It's a need - a must. I hunger and crave for release. I believe art has no limits, boundaries or rules; art rejoices in the mistakes that are made with no clue."

Snow White   2011   60.8 x 91.5 cm.   Smashed glass on canvas

"Art has always come naturally and runs free from my hands, my paintings are colors and shadows as they fade away. It's the smaller things in life that captivate my thoughts. This creativeness becomes an energy, a translucent field connecting the mind and hand. It's the essence of nature that inspires my works."

Nekea Blagoev *Woodland* 2011 178 x 122.5 cm. Acrylic on a concertina

WIL KERNER (1995, Renton, Washington)
Before Wil discovered his art, he spent most of his time watching videos, swinging, and jumping on the trampoline. His unusual interest in colored paper sparked his desire to make cutouts. His cutouts have changed his world. Not only does his family understand him better, but with each piece, Wil is able to share a story and his unique world view. Wil has an exceptional memory, extra-sensory perception, and the uncanny ability to size up people and places. Wil is classified as an autistic savant. His desire to create art is unrelenting - every day he cuts colored paper over and over. Wil's website is www.wilspapercutouts.com.

Party Boy, 2007
20 x 27"
Mixed media

Wil's art is cut from regular construction paper, sulfite construction paper, colored card stock and colored office print stock. Oddly, Wil does not position his fingers and thumb in the holes of his scissors but instead wraps his hand entirely around them mysteriously making them cut.

Wil Kerner *Teeny Toddler* 27 x 20" Mixed media

"*Wil likes to speak in colors. Colors are his verbal interjections providing exclamation about the emotion and meaning of his thinking. He can talk a blue, red, green, orange, purple streak, especially when defining video characters. Since scissors became Wil's constant companion and cutting colored paper his main self-therapy, his reality has blossomed.*" Excerpted from www.wilspapercutouts.com.

TRENT ALTMAN (1977, LOUISVILLE, KENTUCKY)
Trent, an award-winning artist who exhibits nationally in fine art shows and galleries, paints expressionistic abstract pieces in acrylics and mixed media collages on canvas. His work displays an emphasis and commitment to the PROCESS of art over and above the PRODUCT. Creating art has provided Trent connections to peers and friendships, as well as enables Trent to live life with increased independence. Trent is a wonderful example of how someone who has autism has met the challenges to live a full life - both employed at a retail store, and as an artist. Trent lives with a friend who is also his assistant to support independent living. Trent is one of four artists in this book who have been honored with a 2012 United Nations Autism Awareness stamp. Visit Trent's website at www.trentsstudio.com.

An Abstract Flower Garden II   2010   24 x 36"   Acrylic and mixed media
2012 United Nations Autism Awareness stamp selection for World Autism Day

"The viewer of my work is drawn into the wonder of the how, what and why of the process that brought the piece to life. For me, the process of creating rises above all else as I make art to nurture my mind, heart and soul. I reach within myself and share with you my creations."

ANDREW RANDALL (1985, Seekonk, Massachusetts)
Although Andrew has never had an art lesson, he is able to create beautiful and intriguing abstract painting. He typically uses acrylic on canvas, adding sand to the paint because he loves the interesting textures it creates, and the ability it gives him to add dimensions to his work. His method of painting is intuitive; he never uses visual references when he creates. Andrew also has a unique method of brush stroke which results in unpredictable combinations of color and explosive forms of textured paint. Although Andrew's language is limited, it is clear that he paints from his heart and he enjoys the process of creating.

Flight from Chaos   2006   17 x 22"   Acrylic and sand on canvas

Burst, 2007
8 x 10"
Acrylic and sand on canvas

GRANT MANIER (1995, Houston, Texas)

Today's world is evolving into an eco-friendly environment and Grant, an eco-artist, incorporates his passion for conservationism into his work. "Reduce, Reuse and Recycle" is the foundation for Grant's art. Grant creates works of art using magazines, calendars, wallpaper, posters, food wrappers, puzzles and more. Each work contains thousands of cut or torn pieces of recycled paper. Grant likes to call his artwork "COOLAGES." Grant, a captivating young artist and a spokesperson for autism won the Houston's Mayor's Youth Award in 2011 for his activism in the community. Grant's story and art can be viewed at www.GrantsEcoArt.com.

This butterfly is made with recycled puzzle pieces, wall paper, poster board, and acrylic paint. It uses over 1,500 pieces of recycled material.

Puzzled Butterfly, 2010
20 x 16"
Mixed media

"My autism is an art ... I've become a voice for those you cannot hear and I lead by example for those you cannot understand. My mother helped me to express my genius early in life. Now, I am doing my part to teach environmental responsibility and raising the awareness of autism and extraordinary talents through my gift as an Eco-Impressionist."

Grant Manier
Appaloosa, 2011
30 x 24"
Mixed media

At the age of seven, Grant's behavior of repetitively tearing paper was a way of comforting his anxiety and tuning out. Others may have seen this as Obsessive Compulsive Disorder and a behavior to eliminate. However, Grant's mom, Julie, never discouraged this repetitive behavior. In fact, she found it soothing to see him orchestrate the pieces into piles and colors with ease. After a couple of years this behavior became dormant. In adolescence, Grant's paper tearing reappeared. He started his recycling passion as part of a home school project. Combining recycling with paper tearing led to his unique form of Eco-Art. The Appaloosa on this page has over 6,000 pieces of recycled material and took Grant over 130 hours to create. The Appaloosa is the 2011 Austin Rodeo Eco-Art Grand Champion. Grant loves this horse (Dhan Zhao) which he rides weekly as part of equestrian therapy.

GILBERT DAWSON (1980, Cheyenne, Wyoming)
Gilbert received a football scholarship to the University of Nebraska. During that time, he discovered weight lifting and was Lifter of the Year for 2001. After damaging his ligaments, he delved into art, music, poetry, and production. Gilbert has created a style of art he calls Elefunctionism - electrical functioning subconscious breath properties applied to art. *"An elefunctionist has multiple genre talent and approaches life beyond art with a subconscious fire. We reject contemporary art because it doesn't apply to us."* Gilbert's unique books of art and poetry can be purchased on Lulu.com.

"Having AUTISM IS AWESOME, I have never once been stifled in the things I've chosen. My life is pure honest beautiful painting on poetry . . . I have absolutely no complaints."

She Walked Over Opal Cities
and Set his Eyes Free on Fire, 2010
48 x 32"
Oil

"I flunked Kindergarten because I didn't know how to talk to people . . . stuck in a world of dreams, ideas, and glue eating. I was relocated to the therapeutic learning center (TLC) part of the school. My class was composed of four people . . . one deaf, one in a wheel chair, a kid with an abusive family who had temper problems, and me. Now, I know what your thinking; sounds pretty crappy, right? . . . wrong . . . it was amazing. I didn't have to learn things I have no interest in. I was allowed to do puzzles after my spelling, English, and math homework, which usually ended at 10:30 AM. I excelled at putting these creations together; absolutely in love with the picture unfolding before my eyes."

KEVIN COOKE (1985, Lyndhurst, New Jersey)
Kevin, who started painting at the age of 22, is a connoisseur of rock music. He is soft-spoken with a great sense of humor. Kevin participates in the JSDD's Wellness Arts Enrichment Program. Kevin was in the first *Art of Autism* book and has had his art featured in New Jersey and New York shows. Kevin's bold strokes, vibrant color choices and the incorporation of different textures into his work, have Kevin ever-growing as an artist in powerful ways.

Untitled, 2010
23 x 39"
Acrylic and mixed media on canvas

"Painting makes me happy. The colors are excellent and beautiful. I feel excited when people see my art."

KEVIN HOSSEINI (1994, Carpinteria, Calfiornia)
Kevin began painting at age nine when introduced to art by his behaviorist, Colin. Art has become very important to Kevin and serves as a means of sensory fulfillment. It has been the only activity that he has consistently maintained over the years and has helped him through the difficulties he experienced during adolescence. Kevin's art has been influenced by his travels to different countries. In 2011, he was the Naturally Autistic (ANCA) winner for artists aged eighteen and under and participated in a Neurodiversity exhibit at the Museum of Modern Art in the Ukraine. More of Kevin's work can be seen at www.kevingallery.com.

Flowers in Bloom   2011   24 x 30"   Acrylic on canvas

"Kevin has no attachment to the paintings he paints. Once the painting is complete, he doesn't like to talk about it or explain what it is or how he created it. It's finished and he's on to the next painting."   Debra Hosseini, Kevin's mom

Kevin Hosseini *Cow* 18 x 24" Acrylic on canvas

"During adolescence we walked through dark times with Kevin. At that time, I did not know if he would continue his art or what would happen to him. I feared that we had lost Kevin completely to psychosis. I want other parents to know that the dark times will pass. Kevin is now a Junior in High School. Those who know Kevin realize that he has a wonderful sense of humor and a unique perspective of the world.

"Kevin enjoys the sensory input of paint on brush, brush on canvas, and creating swirls of color. He loves texture and thick paint. When we take Kevin to museums and art galleries he's most impressed with artists who use lots of texture. He still stands before the paintings of the Great Masters - Cezanne, Van Gogh, and Matisse - and tries to emulate their brush strokes. The subject isn't as important as the textures, colors, and shapes he sees in the paintings."

Debra Hosseini, Kevin's mom

GRACE GOAD (1994, Nashville, Tennessee)
Grace began painting at the age of four, a year after her diagnosis of moderately severe autism with intellectual disAbilities and a severe speech and language disorder. Her advanced use of color and composition has been featured on the 2007 autism episode of ABC's *The View*, on the cover of *The American Journal of Psychiatry* (Nov. 2010) and the cover of the book *Making Sense of Autism*. Her work is among the permanent Tennessee artists collection at the Tennessee State Museum. She has shown in a variety of venues in Nashville, Soho and Seattle. She can be found online at www.GraceGoad.com.

Untitled Landsacpe 2010 17 x 14" Acrylic on canvas

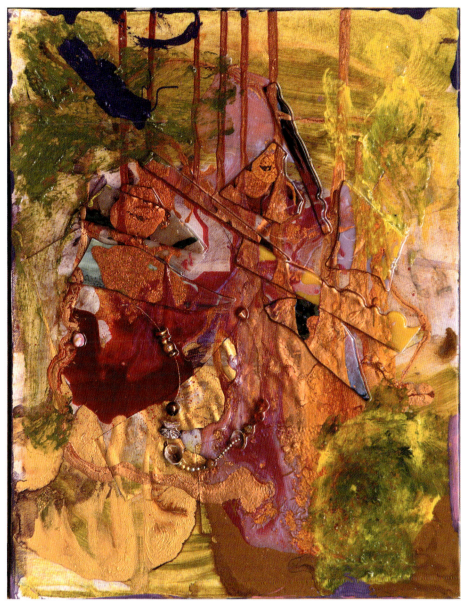

Grace Goad *Puzzle* 2007 19 x 17" Mixed media on paper

"Since she was eighteen months, Grace has been attached to objects, especially something hard, yet slightly pliable to hold in her hand—perhaps fulfilling the common autism sensory need for deep pressure. She's always had a compulsion for collecting and holding things. So, it's natural that her work is often three-dimensional. Putting leaves into her work has been a recurring theme, but one, akin to the color and composition of her work - that is very intentional. Once she plucked a Gingko leaf, saved it and then weeks later, painted it and placed it on a semi-representational piece. In Multimedia Collage V, Grace strung tiny objects onto a wire. She lacks motor strength in her palms, which means she has great difficulty with handwriting and basically does little of it. That is also perhaps why her art is mostly abstract."

Leisa Hammett, Grace's mom

My Voice is my Power

May I present   yes, in a language of words,   but still hear it's truth, the breadth, the colors
           O Please Will U Hear   what must be Heard

                        Hi ! (: wave)
                    hi
My voice is **hi**   My Voice is L$_{OW}$
       It's clamped   & swallowed

   My voice is a kid   It's insecure.   nervous,   & got *quivvers*.

         There's Such GRIEF !   & **RESOUNDS**
My Voice   & all it sounds.
              Strong,   My Voice is my Power,

              My gift   my soul   my heart -
         I'm here to tell   what must be told.

   It Goes aw*ay*   Ashamed   Confused   En*RAGE*d
                     or **BOOMS**

Sometimes I'm worried you   won't enjoy my voice.
          But really there's times I hold back   -   from sharing so,   CORE   me.
(psssh)   to hold back..   neither I nor others enjoy that as much.

              My voice,   even as   ...

  ...   Silent,   ...   - is my Power,
                 Is My Power
                          My Voice

BRIAN BERNARD (1973, Denver, Colorado)
A creative artist since he can remember, Brian is a performer, singer, songwriter, photographer, videographer and more. Visit his art page at www.charg.org/Brian_Bernard_Art.htm. Live and interactive arts is a passion that transforms his senses into his most tenable connection to any reality.

  "Voicing as Calling is an especially precious relationship, based on the inner and outer voice, that brings me wondrous multi-sensory fulfillment. 'My Voice Is My Power' is a spoken word/melody I created for a voice movement class in 2006. I used the top of it to audition and was cast in 'The Elephant Man,' in 2012 with Phamaly.org.

  "Knowing about Asperger's has truly survived me. Otherwise, I'd still be sprinting my strengths only to end up agape and enswamped, again in wonderment at my anomolies. Instead of more judgments, conjecture & calloused graciousness,   Now I grow. More free. To be. Me."

CONNECTIONS

Bryce Merlin *Friends*

"I've brought you a new friend. Please be kind to him and teach him all he needs to know."   Nursery Fairy, *Velveteen Rabbit*

LOUISA JENSEN (1989, Brisbane, Australia)
Louisa lives with her mom, dad, younger brother and three sisters. She was two when she was diagnosed with autism and dyspraxia. From age four, she was taught to communicate via Facilitated Communication. Throughout school she required a facilitator to work with her giving her direct hand support. Since high school, she has become more independent, now only needing support on her arm and shoulder. She uses a variety of communication devices including an IPAD, a letterboard, and a laptop.

The Importance of Facilitated Communication to Louisa Jensen

"Autism is a camouflage to a mind that thinks and says intelligent things, and a body forced to look and behave in strange ways. I can't communicate by speaking because of my lack of control over my movements. That doesn't mean I don't have anything to say! Facilitated Communication gives me more control over my movements so I can point to, and spell out, what I want to say. It gets my thoughts out but is much slower than speech. However, I can show that I do understand lots of things and have answers for many people about life with autism.

"Once I could prove that I have my own thoughts and answers, I was able to go to regular schools with the support of trained facilitators. In high school, I had the opportunity to study all mainstream subjects, selecting as a Senior those subjects that were most interesting and important to me. I graduated in Modern History, Pre-vocational Mathematics and Communication English.

"Since finishing High School, I have had many opportunities to grow in my experiences, as long as I have the support I need. I was able to join a creative writing group where I could develop my skills in writing poems on many topics. Writing poetry to express my ideas is something I really enjoy doing.

"I've always wanted to help people understand that life for a nonverbal autistic person is not how it seems. I want to inspire and make a difference in other people's lives. I believe that I can educate people about life behind the wall of autism. These hopes and beliefs have driven me towards establishing a motivational speaking business where I deliver presentations about my life experiences. The response I receive is very encouraging and it is a wonderful opportunity to help others to understand and respect people with disabilities."

"Autism is a camouflage to a mind that thinks and says intelligent things, and a body forced to look and behave in strange ways. I cannot communicate by speaking because of my lack of control over my movements. That doesn't mean I don't have anything to say!"

MY OBSESSIONS

Louisa Jensen

My obsessions are the driving force in my life
They get my mind in their power,
And they get my life in their power.
My obsessions drive my whole life all at once
So that only obsessions free my obsessive thoughts
Until next time.

Life ruled by obsessive thoughts
Of coke, and having food in my mouth,
Belies the fact that life has other things in it
Because coke is all I can think about.
'Coke and Food and Coke and Food
And Getting Something in its Proper Place'
Has to hold my mind in its grip.

Humans shouldn't get obsessions
Because they are human.
But I am not human
Because I get obsessions.
Not only about Coke and food and getting things away,
But about getting my life back in order again.

How can I get my life in order
When I can't get aide time?
When I can't get help?
When I have obsessions?
When nothing seems to be working good for me?
Can anyone help me?
Does anyone care?
That home has become a home for the angry girl
Who is ruled by her obsessions.

Dear Lord help me to have the great looking girl back that lived here before,
Not the obsessed one that is driving everyone crazy.

BRYCE MERLIN (1981, Central Ohio)
For Bryce, family, friends, pets and celebrities are his favorite subjects to draw. Bryce started drawing these characters at age fourteen. He received a grant from the Ohio Arts Council to publish a book of stories, *Notes from Ohio*. Bryce sells his work at the Heart-to-Art Galleria in Marietta, Ohio, as well as through the Art of Autism shows. Bryce's characters are a way to muse on family and friends and serves as a means of connecting with others when they see and comment on his work. *"I like to draw and decorate in my own way, not the way someone else would."*

Self-Portrait, 2010
28 x 11"
Pen & crayons

"Bryce was a very creative child and had many materials and opportunities for creative play when young. Art leveled the playing field for him and gave him tools of expression that transcended the limitations of his body and mind. When he entered his teens and life became even more challenging for him -- when it seemed that he might be denied a happy life at all -- he came through the other side and so did those who love him. The darkness lasted a long time, but it did pass, and my son emerged with more creativity than ever. Now others are appreciating his unique view on the world as well. He writes and draws and beads and keeps scrapbooks and paints, covering every beloved surface is his individual mission statement: to document the world as he sees it, to hold it close and never lose it, to let us know he loves us back."
                                        Janice Phelps Williams, Bryce's mom

Bryce Merlin
Sara with Bird, 2005
11 x 14"
Pen and crayons

"I had mistakenly thought, years ago, that Bryce would reach age eighteen or twenty and that would reveal the outer boundary of his abilities from which the rest of his life would be lived. At times it was impossible for me to even imagine what life would be like for him as an adult. But I was short-sighted, my dreams for him hidden by what I could only see at the time. His cognitive ability, understanding of actions and consequences, and the ability to be empathetic and see the other-ness of family members -- his ability to wait for dreams to come true and to hold on when it seems they might not -- have continued to improve with each passing year. He'll be thirty-one this year and I do not think we've seen yet the limits of what he can do and where his creativity might lead. When preconceived ideas about what a person should be like are removed; when appropriate supports are given, when help and love and time and hope are all figured in, life can be sweet and good again, even after years of difficulty."
                                            Janice Phelps Williams, Bryce's mom

KIM MILLER (1998, Oregon)
Kim has been drawing since she was three. Her work has evolved from being a window to a young, functionally nonverbal toddler's imaginings to an outlet of emotion for a well-spoken young lady, exploring her own femininity and humanity. *The Girl Who Spoke with Pictures: Autism Through Art*, is a book by Kim's mom, Eileen Miller, and illustrated by Kim. Kim has gained much recognition through her art, resulting in an appearance on *CNN*. Her website is www.thegirlwhospokewithpictures.com.

"I realize I cannot live without art or creativity; it's as essential as breathing and pumping blood."

This painting developed the day after Kim noticed a tulip that had been torn in half by a previous night's storm.

Bug's Eye View, 2011
16 x 20"
Acrylic

"Most people think that our lives took a turn for a more conventional way of living after Kim developed her talent in art. After all, she had learned to draw, she could express her wants and needs. Nothing could be more further from the truth.

"As a small child, she did not indicate her physical needs in any type of manner or communication system. I never knew when she was hungry. As time went on and she grew into an active nine year old, even though she had developed language, she did not approach me or any other person when seeking help in getting what she required.

"One day while in the kitchen, a paper airplane whizzed past my nose and landed on the floor. It wasn't until later that evening, while picking up the papers from the floor in my nightly tidying ritual, that I found these two drawings. I immediately went to the kitchen where I had placed the airplane hours before and unfolded that paper. There was a message on it. It was her way of telling me she was hungry."

Eileen Miller, author of *The Girl Who Spoke Through Pictures*

NOAH ERENBERG (1970, Isla Vista, California)
Both of Noah's parents are artists who encouraged Noah from an early age to express himself through art. When he was young he would constantly draw. Noah has exhibited his art throughout North America, and he and his art have been featured in many periodicals and newspapers, including *The New York Times*. Noah's paintings are on display internationally in a number of major collections.

Noah's work can be viewed at elenamarysiff.com/noah/.

Universe, 2009
12 x 8.5"
Marking pens, ink, paper, collage

Noah's art serves as a means of social contact with other artists. He doesn't attend exhibitions where the art is created solely by artists with disabilities as he doesn't like the stigma of having his art labelled. Noah looks forward to the social aspect of the "art opening," and enjoys meeting up with his artist friends at these events. Art is the major force for total integration in Noah's life.

"I like abstract paintings because I like bright colors and crazy shapes. This type of art reminds me of hip hop music. It seems as if the shapes come out of my head. Abstract means 'from my head.'"

The Moon   2009   12 x 8.5"   Marking pens, ink paper, collage

This painting and the one on the prior page are based on Hans Christian Anderson's *ABC Poems*.

FORREST SARGENT (1991, Seattle, Washington)
Forrest was born in Tokyo and moved to Seattle when he was three. He had a difficult time growing up because of his inability to communicate. When he was a teenager, the family discovered Rapid Prompting Method which allowed him to communicate through the use of a letterboard. This enabled him to express his desire for a camera which gave him another way of sharing his world with others. Forrest resides in a progressive home for the developmentally disabled. More of Forrest's photographs can be viewed at www.sargentstudios.org. *"I know a lot and I want to share it."*

Sun Up Excite   2011   Photograph

"I think photography is the loveliest art because it shows the truth. It shows the secret beauty in things. Taking pictures, I need to find the hidden light in everything. I want people to get pleasure and reach my mind from my photos."

Forrest Sargent *Heather* 2009 Photograph

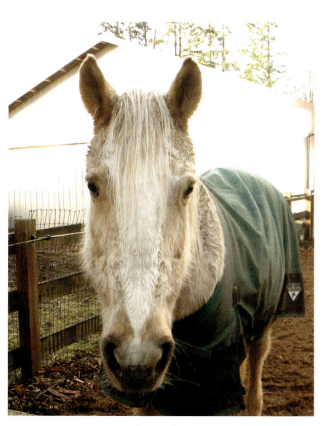

Forrest Sargent *Sir Bosk* 2009 Photograph

    Forrest makes deep connections with horses, like Heather (above). Defying the stereotype that autistic people are uninterested in relationships, one of the first things he told his parents with the letterboard is that he wished he had a girlfriend.
"It makes me feel happy when people see my true self and not just my autism."

STERLING

We are a timeless vapor
Extending over fields of stratosphere
As brilliant as sterling silver
As rooted as the redwood,

We maintain our prism for heavens sake
That the light within us can't be taken,

After years of wordcraft, we are a solitary star
That extends over many moons and maintains balance to the core,
We cannot be hushed nor can we not be noble
When in the fold of discrimination we emerge victorious.

We wear our crimson garments like 5 hearts beating,
With the main heart,
Pleading for the sanity of the rest.

We are the vulnerable blossom that teaches a lesson,
The unspent revelation that logic won't mention,
We are the frost on a field of wheat,
We are the valiant hearts that steady the beat,
We are the poets of this generation.

ERIK ESTABROOK (1984, Alexandria, Virginia)
Erik started writing poetry in the third grade but only became a serious practitioner when he was eighteen. He loves reading Keats and other poets online and sharing experiences and talent through his show on ANCA radio called *The Essence*.

"*I give my parents and the people I meet most of the inspirational credit, but the love and glory I give to God. There's uniqueness in all our lives in that uniqueness is beauty; it's a shame that some people refuse to find what gives them joy and purpose. My poems are not only expressions of me but a guiding light for those who feel abused or unloved. There's not only a purpose for everyone but a gift that everyone has. When we achieve something it's to spread awareness not to make us better than anyone or exalt in proving people wrong.*

"*My poems are not only expressions of me but a guiding light for those who feel abused or unloved.*"

FEELINGS & EMOTIONS

Jonathon Lerman *Untitled*

"The artist is a receptacle for emotions that come from all over the place; from the sky, from the earth, from a scrap of paper, from a passing shape, from a spider's web."
                                                            Pablo Picasso

The Creative Potential of People on the Spectrum

Rebecca McKenzie, Ph.D.

People with autism spectrum conditions have been said to exhibit a lack of creativity and fantasy in thought processes. This perspective is reflected in internationally accepted diagnostic criteria. Psychological measures commonly used to assess the artistic creativity of individuals, are supported by a number of psychological studies which claim that people with autism lack imagination, creativity and the ability to generate novel thoughts. Such studies are clearly based on a limited repertoire of measures, which rely heavily on the assessment of divergent thinking, the ability to generate numerous solutions to a creative 'problem,' often within a limited time span.

The art world provides an alternative perspective on the nature of creative output. In fact, the qualities which lead individuals with autism to perform poorly on psychological measures of creativity are highly valued. Key features of performance by individuals with autism on divergent thinking tasks are: repetition of images with minimal discernible differences; the slow and highly detailed elaboration of one image rather than the rapid creation of many; and, the obsessive expression of images associated with a restricted area of interest. All of these qualities are widely demonstrated in the work of artists who are qualitatively judged by the art community to be exceptional in the creative production of imaginative work.

A recurring theme among many great artists is an obsessive and consuming interest in a particular subject. Paul Cézanne, the 'father of modern art' obsessively pursued an interest in nature. Cézanne's work is characterized by studies of that specific subject over a period of time. Cézanne is certainly far from unique in exploring a particular subject extensively with subtle changes of emphasis in his resulting works of art. Other eminent examples include Monet's lilies, Degas' ballet dancers, Rothko's studies of color fields and Picasso's guitars. Such in depth research-based approaches fall within the traditional practice of artists forming individual bodies of works around one stimulus or another that has caught their obsessive attention.

It has long been known that people with autism have islets of special ability including savant skills in art. The work of artists with autism and related conditions has also been brought to popular attention via the *Outsider Art* movement. Celebrated artists on the spectrum demonstrate highly original, imaginative work expressed through a variety of styles, ranging from realist to abstract.

Observations of creativity among people with autism spectrum conditions are not limited to autistic savants or individuals recognized by the art community. Many parents and practitioners in everyday educational settings also report imaginative and innovative artistic abilities among children and adolescents on the spectrum.

The art community, the inspiring work of individuals with autism, and the reports of practitioners and parents of children with the condition, strongly suggest that there is huge creative potential within this special population. The current diagnostic criteria for autism and related conditions are unrepresentative of these various voices and demand critical review; similarly, based upon evidence from art critics, experts, peers and historical bodies of work commonly used psychological measures of creativity, fail to reflect qualitative assessments.

Dr. Rebecca McKenzie is a developmental psychologist specializing in autism. Rebecca has worked with children, adolescents, and adults with autism spectrum conditions for the last fifteen years. She lectures in the Faculty of Health, Education and Society at Plymouth University, United Kingdom.

A Long-winded Melody

In my head is a long-winded melody

It playfully wafts through my mind

Winding it's way along pathways

Searching for what it might find.

It may spark a long-ago memory

And dance upon peals of laughter

Stopping to dry a falling tear

And each memory that came after.

Wanting to dance, to spin and to prance

I pray that the tune will prompt movement

I readily try lift my arms to the sky

And to force my poor feet off the pavement.

Wanting the tune, a bright balloon

To set my body soaring

To lift on high, my wings to fly

And let my all be adoring.

SYDNEY EDMOND (1992, Temecula, California)
Sydney is the author of several magazine articles and presents at conferences about her communication method, the letterboard. Her poetry has been praised by Temple Grandin, Donna Williams and many others. Sydney has been the subject of a documentary *My Name is Sydney*. At age sixteen, an anthology of Sydney's poetry was compiled in the book *The Purple Tree*.

TIM SHARP (aka Laser Beak Man, 1988, Tingalpa, Australia)
Tim is the creator of super hero Laser Beak Man. Laser Beak Man now has his own animated series showing on ABC3 TV, Cartoon Network Asia, Cartoon Network Australia and Cartoon Network New Zealand. This is a world first for a young autistic man to have his creation turned into a television series screening internationally. Tim's website is www.laserbeakman.com.

The Barbie Que   2010   22 x 33"   Crayon and pen

"Drawing makes me happy. I like meeting people and making them smile with Laser Beak Man."

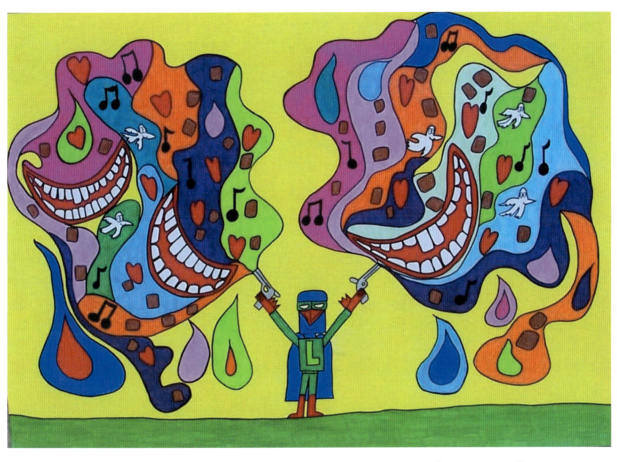

Laser Beak Man *Double Shot of Happiness* 2010 22 x 33" Crayon and pen

Diagnosed with autism at three, the doctor's advice was to "Put Tim away and forget about him." After being told that Tim would never speak, go to school or learn anything, drawing was used to facilitate communication. At age eleven, he invented Laser Beak Man and has been drawing his quirky superhero ever since. Tim's optimistic and colorful drawings communicate his intelligence and wicked sense of humor.

LETTER TO MY FATHER

Dear Dad: have you ever seen the
burning blade, the straight edge of a knife's
tongue? From this, we are branded with bruises. This silence,
this tradition of disguise, is a generational curse,
a baton passed from Grandma to you to
me – and I am still running.

Look at us, Dad. We are made
in digital. I have an older sister that looks like
a broken computer, and another one that looks like
a robot. And you – you look like Data, pieced together with
mud-colored skin, hair like black fizz, and a positronic brain
second to none – but you're different. You'd
tell Picard how to captain his ship. Send Geordi out of the room
while you rebuild the engine of the USS Enterprise out of
old Toyota and Mazda parts. You'd find a way
to make that mutha run on dilithium, even trilithum. The
best engineers in the galaxy would cream themselves
with envy.

But I am paper. An android made out of
the deaths of trees, flattened and bleached. My digital parts
are all up inside my head. You must have known: didn't you ever notice
how my corners would rip when you'd raise the volume of
your voice? But inside, I am
glass. The thing that beats inside of me
is made out of melted sand. I can feel its fractures
when I breathe.

Why do I burn? I am a paper bird. The truth of our

mis-wired brains is a firebrand that I clutch inside my beak

as I fly -- maybe that explains why

I leave a trail of ash behind me as I walk. But my

feathers turned black long ago after I tried to hang

the sun, the moon, and the stars inside every house

that we ever lived in. Do you remember,

Dad? They hung and blazed inside my smile, inside

my scattered Saturday mornings of watercolors and Bob Ross, inside

the piles of books inside my bedroom, inside our trips

to the park where all we needed was lilac blossom, sunshine,

and our hands locked together like transport. But one day,

the stars crumbled, the sun burnt himself inside out and died, and

the moon stopped speaking and disappeared inside

a black hole.

Tell me, how long did we eat our young? The truth is,

we are all glass inside. This is not your fault, Dad; this is

something we learn, something we do as a family. We

tribe of aliens, we Hebrews on Egyptian soil, we of the shattered heart

who will not even dare speak of what makes us strange. I am

just as green and extraterrestrial as

you are, as Grandma was, as those two other sisters

are. But I would like to leave Saturn and live among the natives

in full spectrum color. I have been inside him

for too long.

NICOLE NICHOLSON (1976, Columbus, Ohio)
Nicole was called to poetry as a teenager and has never left. In addition to winning a 2010 Naturally Autistic People Award, her work has been featured in *Poets for Living Waters*, *Qaartsiluni* and in 2011 *Awe in Autism*, on both its website and in its live arts exhibitions. She regularly blogs her poems at *Raven's Wing Poetry* (ravenswingpoetry.com) and writes about her journey with Asperger's Syndrome at *Woman With Aspergers* (womanwithaspergers.wordpress.com). "*I see my poems as a series of 'pictures' that I must translate. 'Letter' speaks to both the genetic inheritance of autism/Asperger's and sometimes the attempts to hide the secret and pretend to be normal.*"

J.A. TAN (1986, Vancouver, British Columbia)
J.A. Tan is a recent graduate of the prestigious Emily Carr University where he received a Bachelor of Fine Arts degree. J.A. is one of four artists in this book to be honored by the United Nations with a 2012 Autism Awareness stamp. More of J.A.'s art can be seen at www.artofjatan.com. *"I've lived all my life in the Philippines but our family became immigrants to Canada in 2005. I began drawing when I was five years old. I would freeze the pictures on the Disney shows I was watching and then I would take my pencil and any paper and draw. I still do that now with my favorite shows."*

Swirling Winds   2009   18 x 24"   Mixed media on canvas

"My favorite artists who influence my art are Monet and Sidney Nolan from Australia. I love art. And even if I have been challenged all these years because of my autism, I always work hard and never give up. My family's support has helped me get to where I am now. So I know I can become a great artist someday. I will continue to work hard and use all the talent I have to achieve my dream."

J.A. Tan
Picasso Inspiration, 2011
36 x 24"
Mixed media on canvas

"I give you my hands
Some filled with joy
Some filled with ache
The weight on my mind
On my shoulders
Keeps me grounded.
I want to fly when I dream
Of the possibilities
When I see the future
The potential actualized
I burst from elation
My sweet realization
This is the significance
I have searched an eternity for
I am revealing my core
Knowing we will all be connected
Indulge me this pleasure
Allow my exposure to be
As part of your soul."

J.A. Tan
The Forest Again, 2011
24 x 36"
Acrylic on canvas

JUSTIN CANHA (1989, Montclair, New Jersey)
Justin is a versatile artist and animator who happens to have autism. His childhood passion for drawing animals and cartoon characters revealed an innate talent that attracted the attention of the mainstream art community when Justin was fourteen years old. Justin is represented by Ricco/Maresca in New York City and has had numerous one-man shows. In 2011, he was featured on the front page of the *New York Times*. A documentary about the friendship of Justin and Lyndsley, his friend in art, is chronicled in a short film called *Sidecars*. A new documentary about Justin and his art is in production. See more of Justin's art at www.justinart.com.

Italian Girl   36 x 24"   Charcoal and oil pastel

"My disability is I'm not going to drive a car because that means no brainstorms."

Justin Canha
Boy Eating Corn, 2006
20 x 30"
Charcoal and pastel on paper

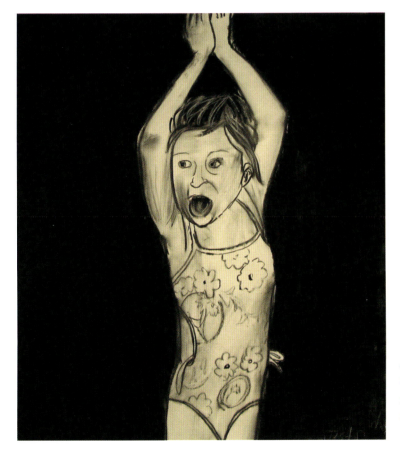

Justin Canha
Girl in a Swimsuit, 2008
30 x 20"
Charcoal and pastel on paper

"My goal is I want to be a famous animator and an illustrator."

MARIA ILIOU (1965, West Babylon, New York)
Maria is an award-winning Greek-American artist and poet. She feels her autism has equipped her to have a deeper, more unique and more varied experience of her life. Her daughter, Athena, also on the spectrum, has a talent for abstract art as well. Maria is active in her community and operates her own freelance autism group, Athena Autistic Artist. Maria also has her own radio show on the ANCA radio network and is an ANCA award winner.

RAG DOLL

Maria Iliou
Athena Iliou

Rag dolls marching to the rainbow

Soaring through beautiful colors
Embracing my rag doll...poetic hugs

Loving memories...overpowering my emotions

Touches heart of my soul

Blue Faces, 2003
14 x 11"
Oil pencils and paint

PURPLE CLOUD

Autistic social situations...extremely anxious
Floating words...disappear in air
Awkwardness of families and friends, uncomfortable
Autistic person, expectations dashed...purple cloud, sad cloud

Cravings of wanting to fit-in, social conversation
Searching for perfect words...connection
Disappointment... here goes another purple cloud

Inappropriate laughter, surfacing...sensory issues
Overwhelming sensation, not knowing what to say or
how others will interpret, or respect you

Unappreciated our gifts of talents and abilities
People have no patience for listening
Missing important information, difficulty appreciating and accepting

People on Autism Spectrum...unique in their eccentric ways
Avoiding changes extremely rigid...covet their daily routines
Brain processing challenges as our body matures

Extraordinary friends confide in, trust with supports
Memories of growth...helps futures confidence
Educating awareness...wisdom of experience
Autism...purple cloud to some

God's gift to others

Maria Iliou

Maria Iliou
Beach at Cape Cod, 2010
14 x 18"
Acrylic

BEAUTIFUL SONG

When you are dancing to a beautiful song
It feels like it is written just for you to perform it
Here you are to express it
So carefully
So gracefully
So beautifully
Every emotion felt
Captivating the audience
As they feel their heart begin to melt
Your sense of balance heightens
As you try and stay steady
You say to yourself
"This is me, I am ready!"
You can feel the muscles in your legs and feet grow stronger
As you perform every leap with bounding power
The intensity rises as you twirl
Dodging the emotions of the song
Which are blowing around you in circles
The audience watches every movement
As you dance in the air
Their emotions run deep
Like they are with you there
You can feel this burning passion and fire in your heart to perform
Just like dancing in the wind
You're the lightning in a storm
Which bolts onto the ocean
And the entire floor lights up around you
After the storm has passed
It feels like you are dancing until the sunset
All around you is of an orange glow
And the audience is your horizon line

SARAH THOMPSON (1984, Charleston, South Carolina)
Sarah loves writing poems that inspire and motivate people. She was diagnosed at age twenty-five with Asperger's. Sarah is married and loves the beach, surfing, dancing, gymnastics, and photography. She would like to write a book which would include her poems and beach-themed photography.

OCTOBER SURF

Out here I know my life won't pass me by
I can live my life to the fullest
I enjoy the challenge of it all
Even though I am challenged
I still feel so happy
Any fears I have out here
Just make me feel more alive
My life is real
My heart, it beats
The water is cold
My life won't pass me by

Sarah Thompson

Sarah Thompson
In the Waves, 2011
9 x 12"
Crayons melted on canvas

GUY MCDONNELL (1989, Seattle, Washington)

Guy, diagnosed with autism at age three, recovered from a brain stroke and surgery at age twelve. In the summer of 2008, Guy began painting abstract art. He enjoys the colors, motions, and satisfaction from start to finish. He has displayed his work at a number of art walks and is currently represented by *HeART of the Spectrum* art gallery in Seattle.

Guy's goals are to have his art in public places and to use his art for integration into the community. His mom, Malinda, hopes to create a respite art program out of their studio for friends.

Love in Action   2011   24 x 36" Acrylic

"My artist statement would best be a picture of me swinging in the rain, or snow, or sunshine in the beautiful city I love, Seattle! My favorite parks are Sandel, Carkeek and Discovery where I go to be outside, to hike and get fresh air every day. I like to paint like I play, full of action."

Guy McDonnell *Morning* 2011 40 x 30" Acrylic

JONATHAN LERMAN (1987, Newark Valley, New York). Jonathan's extraordinary art talent emerged quite suddenly at the age of ten. Jonathan's early drawings *"were a means of giving order to and assembling his fragmented visual world."* Jonathan is one of the only artists in this book who draws primarily faces and interactions between people - lovers, mothers and babies. He had his first solo exhibition at the KS Art Gallery in New York in 1999, when he was only twelve years old. He has since gained international recognition for his art.

Jonathan Lerman   *Untitled #37*   2007   24 x 19"   Charcoal on bristol board

Jonathan's art spontaneously emerged at age ten shortly after his maternal grandfather died. Caren, his mom, believes the timing was significant and that the grandfather was somehow communicating through her son's art.

PASSIONS

Kevin Hosseini *Tango*

"Man is only great when he acts from passion."
Benjamin Disraeli

TONGUE IN CHEEK

Ice skates.

Somewhere along the way, we took them off. I'm not sure when. I remember Brittany saying she was hungry, and then I realized I was, too. We found the boys, still gliding around the rink, and waved for them to come over

And then Ryan was standing there, and now my hands are clammy and I'm fumbling with the laces on my skates. He smiled at me. Can you believe it? He's absolutely the cutest guy I've ever seen, and I feel like we're so connected. He just, he really understands me, you know? It's so hard to hang out sometimes, though, because his mom doesn't like me. I don't know. Just because I'm seventeen and he's fourteen, there's nothing wrong with that. He's really mature for his age, too, and I don't understand why she doesn't see that.

Now he's looking at me, offering a hand as I grab the slices of pizza and sodas for our table. How sweet! I can't get over how thoughtful he is. I grab the plastic knife, dutifully scraping off the yards of melted mozzarella from atop my slice, leaving it in a heap on the plate. Normally everyone says how gross it is, and that I must be crazy or stupid to take the cheese off.

But not Ryan.

Brittany is talking to Robbie about something, and the next thing I know, she's telling us we should play Truth or Dare. Oh, God, I don't like that game. What if I get dared to do something stupid, or unpleasant, or that I just plain won't understand how to do? My stomach is in knots already, even though it's not my turn right now, but Ryan's.

"I dare you...to French kiss Amy."

WHAT?

The words have just come out of Brittany's mouth, but I'm not sure if I really heard them. She always says I'm obsessed with Ryan, and now this. What does it mean? My cheeks are flushed and red, and I have no idea what to do or say. How do we do this? When? Should we go somewhere? Does she expect him to do it right here, at the table?

As if sensing my apprehension and unease, he stands up then.

"Come on," he says, nodding his head towards the bank of grey lockers a short distance away.

I follow him on unsteady legs, willing my knees to remain upright enough so that I look at least somewhat composed. The hand clamminess from earlier has graduated to sweatiness, and I wipe my palms on my jeans as we come to a stop in front of the lockers, in a more private area, out of our friends' line of sight.

I'm concentrating on rhythm—the slow rise and fall of my chest, and my heart pounding underneath. For a few moments, we just stand there, neither of us sure what to do next. Finally, he takes a deep breath, stepping closer to me, close enough to where I can feel the heat coming off of him and inhale the musk of some overly-strong cologne he's wearing.

"Ready?" he asks.

I nod.

He presses his lips to mine, and I'm frozen. I wonder if I should close my eyes or leave them open, but I see him close his and take the hint. So...now what? Oh, wait a minute... there's his tongue. I can feel it between my lips, moving past my teeth into the cavern of my mouth, and whoa, I have never felt anything like this before.

Hmm...this is supposed to feel good, isn't it? Maybe I'm not doing it right. I can't believe this is even happening. Why is he kissing me, anyway? I know he likes that girl Nicole. She's much prettier and smarter than I am and probably a way better kisser, so he'll end up with her anyway.

I could never be good enough for him.

He breaks the kiss then, and I gasp as we both pull back for air. We both stay still for a moment, trying to catch our breath, and my lips are still tingling slightly with the memory of our kiss.

"Well, okay, so we did that," I blurt, not noticing the flush of crimson on his cheeks. "Let's go back to the table now."

"Okay."

I'm walking in front of him, unaware of his downcast eyes behind me, my own head held high and proud. Our friends acknowledge our return with applause and cheers, and I am unable to stop the spread of the happy grin across my face. As we settle back into our seats, I look over at Ryan again, hoping that the message in my eyes is loud and clear: *Thank you.*

AMY GRAVINO (1983, Montclair, New Jersey)
The little girl at the typewriter is smiling - eyes wide, cheeks red and high with the joy only youth can possess. Someday, she will have the words. Someday, she will write, and her gift will become a gift to others. Starting with poems at age ten, then short stories, and now a book chronicling her experiences with dating, romance, and sexuality as a young woman with Asperger's Syndrome, Amy does not write because she wants to, but because it is something that comes from within and flows out of her. Once described as "a hilarious and painfully honest combination of Ernest Hemingway and Erma Bombeck," Amy is using her writing, public speaking, and most recently, her work as a college coach to change the lives of individuals on the autism spectrum.

DR. TEMPLE GRANDIN (1947, Fort Collins, Colorado)
Dr. Grandin is the best known living person with autism. She's an expert on livestock behavior, designer of livestock handling facilities and Professor of Animal Science at Colorado State University. She has designed livestock facilities in the U.S., Canada, Europe, Mexico, Australia, New Zealand and other countries. Dr. Grandin received her Ph.D. in Animal Science from the University of Illinois in 1989. She is the author of many books and the subject of a recent HBO movie.

"When I was a child, art was my favorite subject in school. My parents always encouraged my ability in art. Half of the cattle in the United States are handled in facilities I designed. Being a visual thinker really helped me in my design work. In my book 'Thinking in Pictures,' I explain how words narrate the videos in my imagination. When I design equipment I can test run it in my mind like a three-dimensional virtual reality system. I owe my success to my mother and good teachers. When I was goofing off in high school, my science teacher got me interested in studying so I could be a scientist. Abilities have to be developed. It took me three years of hard work to learn how to design cattle handling facilities. I encourage teachers, parents, and individuals on the spectrum to work on developing strengths that can be turned into good careers."

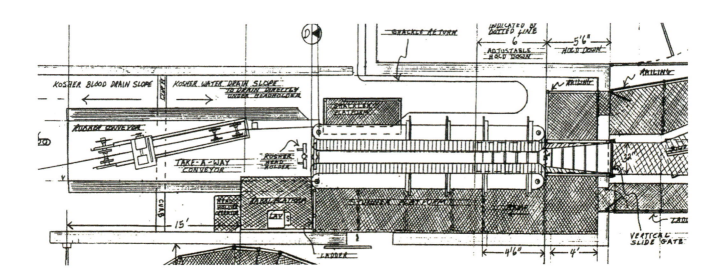

Temple Grandin has designed many systems for the humane and efficient handling of cattle. Her systems take advantage of the natural behavior of cattle to circle back from where they've come from. Above is a detail of the blueprint *Typical Restrainer System for Kosher Slaughter* designed in 1984.

TREVOR AYCOX (1995, Healdton, Oklahoma)
Trevor took up painting in 2007, when he was twelve. He became fascinated with an artist in Galveston who used spray cans to paint. He quickly learned the craft and now performs all over the United States. In 2010, he won a scholarship from Assembly of God Fine Arts Festival and the following year he was a state finalist for the Scholastic Art and Writing Awards. In 2011, Trevor travelled to many locations with the *Art of Autism* and *Awe in Autism* shows.

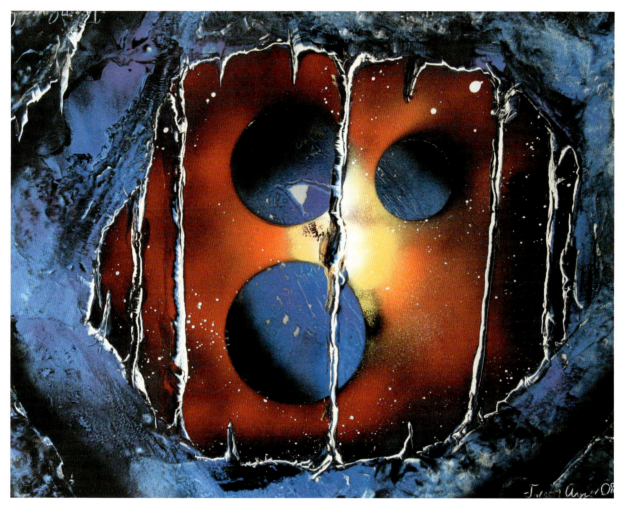

Trevor Aycox   *Deep Caverns*   2008   14 x 17"   Spray paint on posterboard

"Sometimes I feel like autism limits me in some things, especially when social skills are important. When I do my art, I see what I can really do. I'm not very good at things like sports that are important around here. It makes me feel good about myself to go past the limits that are set by either me or other people. I try hard not to let autism keep me from doing what I want to do."

MARCY DEUTSCH (1983, Yelm, Washington)
When Marcy was diagnosed with autism at age five, doctors told her parents Marcy would never go to college, never make friends and that she would require placement in an institution or group home when she became an adult. She defied the odds and graduated from a two-year college with honors. She even learned to fly airplanes! Marcy has created her own successful business selling her art creations. She speaks publicly about her journey and inspires many with her story. Marcy's website is www.critteronthings.com.

African Wildlife   2003   21 x 25"   Colored pencils

"I draw animals because I love them and I connect to the world through them."

Marcy Deutsch *African Elephant* 2007 11 x 8.5" Colored pencil

GABRIEL PREBOY (1982, Toronto, Canada)

Gabriel is a self-taught artist who exhibited a prodigious talent for drawing at an early age. His first obsession was buses at age two, and he drew them regulary and well. When he was three he became fixated on dinosaurs and read every children's book available on the subject. His parents published a book of his drawings titled *Gabriel's Dinosaurs*, which sold out in retail stores. Professional publishers declined to publish it because they mistakenly thought a four-year-old could not have achieved such a remarkable accomplishment unless forced by his parents to do so. The truth is, that Gabriel has been drawing - calmly, consistently and patiently - for most of his life. His calm, graceful, and clear demeanor coupled with his remarkable focus have made him a prolific artist. Gabriel has the unique ability to render his drawings effortlessly on the page, no matter how large or small, without using formal meauring techniques.

Golden Eagle, 2010
22 x 10"
Graphite on paper

Southern Cassowary, 2010
22 x 10"
Graphite on paper

Gabriel has been drawn to various subjects over the years, though birds and animals, as well as the supernatural, have been his preferred focus. In 2010, he drew a series of about 75 birds inspired by a book of colored photographs entitled *Extraordinary Birds*. These two images come from that collection. In 2011, he concerned himself with a series of spacescapes from his imagination, and presently he's working on paid commissions - rendered drawings from photographs of people, pets, places and things. All who know Gabriel, expect his art to continue to evolve as he matures.

SHEILA MAHON (1954, Ojai, California)

Sheila was born in New Jersey and lived as a young child in Mexico. Sheila paints, makes jewelry, and enjoys mosaics and pottery. Some of her favorite subjects are drums, animals and angels. Sheila lives and works in Ojai where she is active in the community.

Angel 1   2011   Mixed media

Angel 2   2011   Mixed media

Sheila can instantaneously and accurately tell the day of the week given the date of a person's birth.

JASON CANTU (1985, Morro Bay, California)
Graduating with honors from high school in 2004, Jason went on to graduate from Cuesta College in San Luis Obispo, California. His focus of study has been primarily art. Jason has won awards for his work and sold his art at student shows at Cuesta College. He works in a variety of mediums and has incorporated computer graphics into his repertoire. He hopes to have a one-man show of his art work in 2012.

"In my early years, I always liked to draw maps and draw on old maps, making new freeways, all the different interchanges, on-ramps and off-ramps, really intrigued me from a curiosity standpoint. I still currently draw maps on occasion, but it's more from a purely artistic standpoint, when I feel there's something I can contribute to the art."

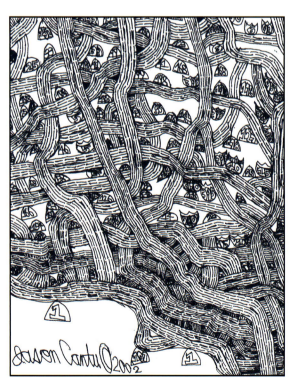

Untitled Map
11 x 8.5"
Pen and ink

Bunch of Freeways, 2002
11 x 8.5"
Pen and ink

Jason Cantu *Innocence Lost* 2011 24 x 18" Charcoal

CANDACE "CANDY" WATERS (2000, Park Ridge, Illinois) Candy is a beautiful redheaded girl who likes painting, music, swinging, playing in the water, jumping and pizza. Candy was honored in 2008 by the Mayor of Park Ridge, Illinois, when he hung one of her paintings in the foyer at City Hall. Candy's favorite thing to paint is the sun. Her paintings have sold at auctions benefiting autism organizations. She is the inspiration for the radio program *The Candy Store*. *The Candy Store* can be heard on www.blogtalkradio.com/thecandystore.

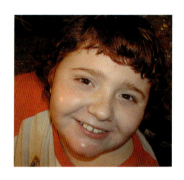

Mr. Sun   2008   24 x 30" Tempura paint on canvas

Candace is the inspiration for the song *Faith, Love and Hope*. Her song has influenced and inspired politicians, autism organizations, and most importantly, parents around the world.

ISABEL BROKAW (1992, Preston, Connecticut)
Ever since she was little, Isabel has enjoyed the arts and computers. Over the years, she has drawn hundreds of characters, especially favoring dragons of her own creation, which she composes stories about. Isabel will sketch her images, scan them into the computer, and digitally enhance them to her liking. Her interests are animals, Anime, mangas, Pokemon, dragons, and her own story characters from her dream world, Ninsense. Isabel writes brilliant imaginative stories, and is an expert on dragons.

The Rage Within
2010
Digital media

Wrath and Pride
2011
Digital media

FLORENTINA (1997, Ojai, California)

Florentina is an amazingly creative soul who entered this world on a train in Romania. At three years of age, she met her mom, who brought her to the USA. At four, she was diagnosed with an immune system dysfunction and autism. Florentina receives her inspiration from her experiences in interrelating with the world around her. Through her art she has been expressing her life journey since she was four. She is known for her intuitive spirit, artist soul and pure love of life. An eclectic artist, she will move from painting with acrylics to creating intricate colorful abstracts with a computer paint program; which she taught to herself. Other mediums she uses are crayon, color pencil and pen.

Stripes: My Stripes May Be Different But My Heart Beats the Same
2008   9 x 11" Crayon

"I'm often asked if Florentina has any help creating her art. She doesn't. She's self-taught in all mediums, including computer art. She's had no mentors; no one standing behind her telling her what to do or offering suggestions. In fact, she'll tell you to stop and go away. Everything she creates comes from her; her heart, her life experiences. She's not a savant; she's an artist, simple as that."

Andrea Clarke, Florentina's mom

KRISTEN MOINICKEN (1990, Apple Valley, Minnesota)
When Kristen began to attend school, her teachers immediately noticed her intelligence and creative abilities. At an early age, she became intensely interested in dinosaurs, prehistoric creatures, ocean life and dragons. In the third grade, she was diagnosed with Asperger's syndrome. Kristen loves drawing and creating mixed media artwork combining materials like Sculpey, fabric, beads, wire and paper. An animal lover, Kristen decided to become a vegetarian several years ago.

Untitled, 2011
Pen & colored pencil

"I think having Asperger's syndrome makes it both easier and harder for me to draw. I am able to focus on my artwork and really get involved with it, but I always need to be alone when I draw. I feel uncomfortable if someone watches me when I create art."

WILDFIRE

It's like a raging wildfire.
No one knows exactly when or where it started,
But it didn't start on its own.
It started with a tiny flick of disrespect.
Perhaps unintentional, or perhaps through
An act of ignorance
But either way, it went unnoticed.
Ignored, uncared for and forgotten.
Until it caught on and spread.
Freely dancing flames.
Slowly, at first,
As if unsure of where to go next.
Then it found its way.
Racing and roaring in all directions.
Trying to catch up to the source of its creator.
Destroying anything that may get in its way.
Pain and suffering of the innocent left behind.
No time! It had to catch up!
Trying to teach a lesson.
The lesson of respect and love and care.
Until it looked back, if only for a moment,
To see the very same lesson it had failed to learn itself.
To see its own unintentional disrespect.
And even after it has been controlled,
And innocence once destroyed has been rebuilt,
How can such a hypocritical monster
Ever forgive itself?

ERIN CLEMENS (1989, West Chester, Pennsylvania)
Erin is the 2011 Naturally Autistic (ANCA) award recipient for poetry. She has been writing poetry since she was in the eighth grade. *"To me, my poetry is a way of expression and communication. It is a way to release emotion that is building up inside."*

HOPE

Maximus Oberto *Sunflowers II*

"A diagnosis of autism is not the end of the world ... it's the beginning of a whole new world."   Anonymous

It Takes a Child
Elaine Hall

When traditional therapies didn't help my son Neal, who was adopted from a Russian orphanage at two years old and diagnosed with autism at three, I sought out creative people: actors, writers, artists, and musicians, to work with him. Ten hours a day, seven days a week we followed Neal's lead, connected to him on his terms. We joined his world.

When Neal stared intensely at his hand, we stared at ours. When Neal pounded the floor, we brought out drums and pounded with him. When Neal spun in a circle, we spun with him, round and round for as long as he wanted, until we were all laughing, connecting, daring, relishing our special haven, and our own, unique version of Ring Around the Rosie.

This led to days and experiences that were novel, magical, amazing. Bit by bit, Neal relinquished his solitary world. Gradually, the miracle happened and he merged into another world: Ours.

What worked for Neal has worked with hundreds of children through *The Miracle Project*, a theater arts program for children with autism and other special needs. I grew this program through the collective efforts of creative people who managed to connect with children on the autism spectrum. The premise is that, by joining a child's world without judgment, we form relationships. Through relationships, children can develop everything they need: they can learn to engage with others, communicate with gestures, use ideas creatively, think and reflect.

Why creative people? Simple. Creative types don't need to learn how to think outside the box. Like those with autism, we often don't even know there is a box! Artists are, by nature, non-conformists. What can be more non-conforming than autism?

I've learned so much from Neal and others on the spectrum. I know now how to experience the world with a heightened sensitivity that allows me to appreciate Creation in such a profound way. Simple tasks can take on an almost spiritual quality. For example, there was a time when I tried to go on a walk with Neal and he insisted that we stop at every single hubcap attached to every single car on every street. I used to say, "Come on, let's go." And we'd battle.

One day, I stopped with him, knelt down, and stared at the hubcaps, and I saw the most beautiful thing: the sun falling on a hubcap creates a kaleidoscope of brilliant, shining shards of light. They are magical! After that day, Neal never needed to stop and look at hubcaps again, though I sometimes asked if we could.

There is this myth that children with autism don't have empathy. I've found the exact opposite to be true: children with autism are instead the most highly sensitive individuals I have ever had the privilege to know. They simply express themselves differently. If Neal likes you, he may smell your hair. If he finds you to be insincere, he will walk away or throw something.

Yes, there are the difficult challenges of autism: the tantrums, the delays, the stimming, perseverating, and other frustrations. I don't want to minimize these, yet if we dare look at all behavior as communication, we can see these actions as different forms of communicating.

Perhaps the world is too loud, too fast, too toxic and it's the so-called typical folk who need to take a step back and reflect on what we're doing and how much we may be missing in our world. Perhaps our children with autism are here to teach us to look at the world with a different set of eyes; a new perspective. I've found such immeasurable joy, love, and value in the pure and simple creative connection I have with Neal and others like him.

They say it takes a village to raise a child. I think it takes a child with autism or other special needs to raise the consciousness of a village.

Elaine Hall is the founder of the Miracle Project profiled in *AUTISM: The Musical*. She is the author of *Now I See the Moon* (Harper Collins 2010) and coauthor with Diane Issacs of *Seven Keys to Unlock Autism: Creating Miracles in the Classroom* (Wiley 2011).

ANDREW MENDOZA (1983, Santa Maria, California)

Andrew has been drawing since four. In seventh grade he was diagnosed with Asperger's syndrome after many frustrating years of assessments with no diagnosis. Throughout school, he resisted the ASD diagnosis and had problems with being bullied. It's only recently through participating in events with other artists on the spectrum, he's felt a sense of community and pride. He continues to paint the animals he has a special bond with and has participated in *Art of Autism* shows in California and New York City. *"Sketching and painting has always been an important part of my life growing up. I still enjoy drawing and it is a big part of my life to this*

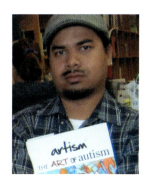

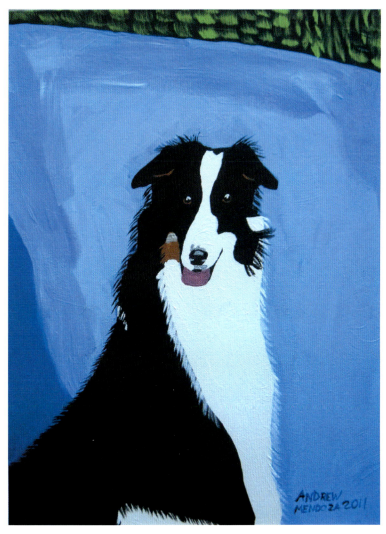

Collie   2011   20 x 16"   Acrylic on canvas

"I attribute Andrew's success to involving him in many programs, including Special Olympics, social skills training, the Special Needs Network, and bowling. His art has always been an important part of his life. I worked one-on-one with Andrew and always included his brothers. Don't think we didn't have difficult times during puberty. Today I'm so proud of Andrew and his continued growth and success. At age 27, he passed his California Driver's exam. He's on his own track."   Rosie Zepeda, Andrew's mom

PAMELA WILLIAMSON (1992, Victoria, British Columbia, Canada)
As a toddler, it was very obvious that Pamela had a keen sense of observation and spatial orientation, even though she had lost her ability to speak at the age of eighteen months. By the time she was five, she was diagnosed with autism and her parents were told she would never go to school, speak, nor recognize her family. Pamela and her parents worked very hard, and by the age of six she was in school, writing stories as well as illustrating them. Pamela developed a love of birds, especially penguins. Today she sketches, paints and uses the computer to produce digital images of animals, birds and whatever else catches her fancy. Pamela graduated from high school in 2011 and is presently attending Victoria College of Art in Victoria, British Columbia. She hopes to become a famous artist one day, one who works with penguins.

Pamela and the Penguins   2010   Digital media

Pamela Williamson *Female Calliope* 2011 Digital media

Pamela Williamson
Macaws, 2011
Digital media

Pamela's parents took her to many museums and art galleries and though Pamela walked through most of them with her hands shading her eyes, looking straight ahead, her fingers in her ears, professing that it was "not for Pamela," she would return home and draw what she had seen through her peripheral vision in minute detail.

Joel with Kyle Negrete

JOEL ANDERSON (1990, San Diego, California)
Joel is an award-winning artist, songwriter, public speaker and philanthropist. He started drawing at the age of five and began painting at eleven. Joel was an award recipient for the 2010 Naturally Autistic Awards. He has been an active volunteer for the Autism Tree Project Foundation and many other charitable organizations. Although Joel has lived only a little more than two decades, he has proven himself to be an inspiration to many. Joel's website is joelsvisionarts.com.

The Mentor Lion   2010   16 x 20"   Acrylic on canvas

Joel participates in a mentorship program through the Autism Tree Foundation and the USD football team. Joel's mentors have become much more than mentors; they are friends and part of Joel's family. Joel once asked his football mentors, Kyle and Ade what their favorite animal was. They both responded "Lion." Joel painted *"The Mentor Lion"* in honor of them.

THE COLORS OF MY MIND

I paint in colors of the rainbow
And I see yellow of the sun,
And blue in the sky.
I know you'll feel fine and smile -
When you see the colors of my mind.

I see joy in green, courage in blue,
Strength in red, love in yellow too
The colors of my mind.

I draw pictures of history
And I see landscapes of adventure,
And characters of mystery.
I know you'll feel fine and smile -
When you see the colors of my mind.

I see joy in green, courage in blue,
Strength in red, and love in yellow too.
I know you'll feel fine and smile -
When you see the colors of my mind.

And when I paint
I feel peace
I can face the world with ease.

I see the world around of artistry
Displaying creativity -
I travel to get this inspiration,
To have another look -
At the colors of my mind.

In 2011, Joel recorded *The Colors of My Mind* and it is available for sale on CDBaby.com. Joel says "the *Colors of My Mind* is why I paint. To see you smile."

The painting to the right is of Joel's mentor Kyle Negrete. Look closely. Joel has painted himself into the front row.

Kyle Negrete, 2011
10 x 8"
Acrylic on canvas

MICHAEL SACHS (1992, Simpsonville, South Carolina)
When he lost the ability to communicate with words, Michael communicated with pictures. He drew with markers, pencils, chalk and a computer mouse - with anything, on anything. Eventually at age four, Michael was diagnosed with autism. From the beginning, art has been Michael's passion. His style today reflects his love of color (especially red), texture, and perspective.

Crazy Cat   2009   16 x 20"   Acrylic on canvas

Michael most enjoys creating acrylic paintings and cartoon representations of his world. He loves to paint flowers, animals, birds, and landscapes. He also enjoys photography and often incorporates his photographs into his drawings.

Michael Sachs *First Day of School* 2011 8.5 x 11" Paper and markers

Though now fully verbal, Michael continues to express emotions, experiences, and interests through his artistic creations.

CHRISTIAN EARLY (1964, Pembroke Pines, Florida)
In 2009, Christian's first illustrated book *Can You See Me?*, became available in bookstores. Painting for Christian did not come easy. Yet, he persevered with encouragement from his mom and teachers and now is an accomplished artist. He sees the world as funny and comical and has a unique sense of humor and laughter that is contagious.

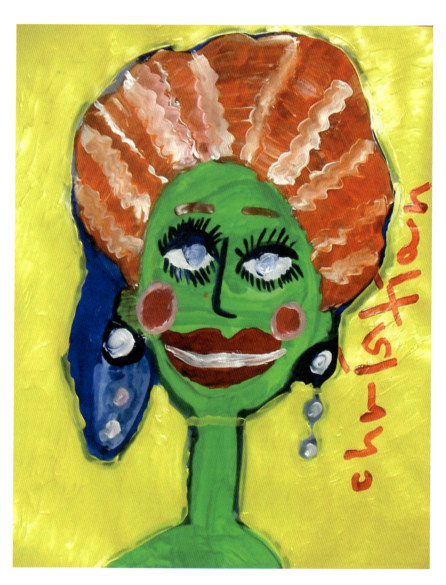

Crazy Lady in Yellow
2008
24 x 19"
Acrylic

"We must shout to provide avenues in art schools, community colleges specializing in creative studies and any such endeavors that pinpoint utilizing the right side of the brain, the creative side, the neglected side in the educational system, the non-verbal side. An option that has not been available to our sons and daughters, but may prove to constitute a different fulfilling future for them. Let us not say after they obtain that 'special diploma' they graduated to nothing."

Mayra Ron, author of *Can You See Me?* mom to Christian Early

BRANDON DRUCKER (1991, Fort Lauderdale, Florida)
Brandon started drawing at age two to communicate his ideas. At three, he was diagnosed with autism and he had limited speech until the age of five. His drawings and the storybooks he continues to create today often reflect the people he has met and places he has visited. He enjoys meeting new people and discovering new places. Brandon is a founding member of Artists with Autism, a south Florida networking group for artists on the spectrum.

Rainbow Boats   2010   9 x 12"   Watercolor

Brandon's mom, Cynthia, says Brandon has more goals and ambition than any person she knows, though he has challenges relating to comprehension. Two years ago he taught himself Spanish by putting the subtitles on the TV and memorizing Spanish songs. He enjoys singing and speaking in public, often ad-libbing. He writes song lyrics in both Spanish and English and records them on his YouTube channel. He's currently writing a Spanish love story, as well as a cartoon series based on a family with a child with autism. His recently developed friendships with two neurotypical boys has changed his life. He feels a new-found sense of acceptance in his social circle and pride in his accomplishments.

DANIEL JOHN SVOBODA (1982, Shaw AFB, South Carolina)
Daniel, who was diagnosed with autism and psychomotor retardation at age three, has overcome his challenges, in part, by creating an imaginary world of friends, Imagiville, and inviting other kids to be part of his vision of the world. More of DJ's characters can be viewed at www.myimagiville.com.

"Each Imagifriend I draw is different. They come in many sizes, colors, and designs. None of them are ever mean or cruel. They each have their own special job and purpose in Imagiville. Every Imagifriend knows as long as they've a kind heart it doesn't matter what they look like. Some of them are physically or mentally handicapped but that's okay. I've just had my first book published too. It's about acceptance and respect for those with autism.

"I want to use The Imagifriends to help others with autism know they are special just the way they are. I've created The Imagifriends coloring book and I do Imaginames. That's where I create an Imagifriend out of the letters of your name and connect them. I donate a portion of what I earn to various autism organizations and to my wonderful church, Hope Community Church. Being autistic has presented me with many challenges in my life. From these challenges I've learned never to give up."

"The Imagifriends of Imagiville are based on the experiences I've faced during times at school. There were days at school when I was made fun of and when I was picked on and treated mean. Those made me feel very sad and hurt. That is how I got the idea of the Imagifriends of Imagiville."

The Mupporezmo, 2007
12 x 8"
Marker and pen

KAYLIN MANGOLD (1996, Colorado Springs, Colorado)
Kaylin first started drawing at age three as a means of communicating her feelings. Due to her delayed speech, she attended a special needs preschool that recognized and fostered her talents as well as helping her work through some of her struggles. Although her parents knew when Kaylin was young that she was unique, they didn't receive a diagnosis of autism until Kaylin was eight. Through many years of hard work and therapy Kaylin is now able to communicate well verbally. The detail and emotion that she's able to show in her art is her true way of sharing her feelings. Kaylin aspires to help teach the world to be a kinder place, and would one day like to design a video game. *"I just want to be able to be myself."*

Toucan Paradise, 2003
12 x 18"
Crayons

Kaylin's favorite quote is from *The Velveteen Rabbit* - *"Love makes us real."*

CARLY HATTON (1992, Ontario, Canada)
Carly's award-winning art has been displayed and sold throughout Canada, England, and the United States. Carly is a published illustrator and writes parodies of movies she watches. She is multi-talented and likes to create cartoons and enjoys making small sculptures. In 2011, Carly's illustrations were featured in *Limericks from the Animal Kingdom*, by I. Mary Hackney. Carly's website is www.CarlysArt.com.

Loan Shark

The white shark with wide gaping jaws
Is a ruffian with many flaws
The human sharks practice
The same business tactics
And bending or breaking of laws.

Limericks from the Animal Kingdom, by I. Mary Hackney,
Illustrated by Carly Hatton (Spiral Press, 2011)

"I love drawing because it's how I express myself, as well as in my writing. It also unleashes my imagination and allows me to explore other types of worlds. Things about myself: I enjoy reading, and of course the drawing and writing... Music and those other things are what help me with my artwork and stories, with its love, family, friendship, feelings, adventure, funny humor and many other kinds of categories."

MAXIMUS OBERTO (2001, Ventura, California)
Overcoming a challenging birth, and enduring endless hours of speech therapy, physical therapy, social skill building sessions and other interventions, Maximus now has the skills to help him express himself verbally. His art and journaling are another form of self-expression, providing Maximus with important outlets and tools to help him better handle feelings of frustration and anger. These areas of growth have helped Maximus to become more comfortable and patient with his teachers, staff and classmates.

Outer Space 2010 12 x 18" Watercolor

"Maximus is shy about his work. His art has been featured in several publications. He says he doesn't like all the attention and doesn't want to become famous. But I know deep down inside he loves it. Especially when he turns away with a giant smile and has a look of pride and accomplishment on his face." — Sunny Oberto, Maximus' mom

THANK YOU

First and foremost, I want to thank the artists, their families, and agents for their patience and cooperation. Special thanks to Elise Blumenthal, Sherry LaMunyon, Rosele Frishwasser, Janice Phelps Williams, Julie Coy, and all the other moms, dads, aunts, uncles, and grandmas I've met through the process of collecting the art. We share our common struggles, successes and stories.

The Art of Autism: Shifting Perceptions is truly a collaborative effort. Many people encouraged and helped me create this book. Keri Bowers a generous friend and fellow autism parent, Kurt Muzikar my partner in life, and Nancy Lea Speer my best friend, all edited and assisted with the layout and design.

I want to express a special thanks to my son, Kevin who inspires me everyday in unexpected and beautiful ways. He has shown me how life can unfold on its own terms and not be limited to the boxes society imposes.

Since the first *Art of Autism* book was printed in 2011, *The Art of Autism* has become more than a book or an event - it's become an exciting movement. Our mission is to create attitudinal and perceptual shifts through collaborations. In 2011 and 2012, we have expanded our group to include many more artists, poets, and entertainers, as well as many like-minded organizations. Thank you to all who participate in our shows and to all the individuals and organizations who support our project. We've listed a number of them and their websites on Page 144.

To our readers, thank you for your interest in the artistic expression of people on the spectrum. We're only beginning to understand the complexity and development of the autistic mind. With this new understanding, my hope is *The Art of Autism* will challenge the reader to ponder the wonder and diversity of human potential, encourage people with new diagnoses to explore their own creativity, and foster support in communities for sustainable art programs.

Debra Hosseini
Carpinteria, California
2012

INDEX

14	Allen, Frank	82	Jensen, Louisa
45, 70	Altman, Trent	68	Kerner, Wil
12	Anderson, Jack Carl	24	LaMunyon, Amanda
132	Anderson, Joel	93, 110	Lerman, Jonathan
22	Antram, Lisa	9, 10	LeProust, Beatrice
42	Avraham, Neri	119	Mahon, Sheila
115	Aycox, Trevor	139	Mangold, Kaylin
32	Azeem, Qazi Fazli	72	Manier, Grant
28	Beck, Gerhard	108	McDonnell, Guy
80	Bernard, Brian	21	McManmon, Michael
66	Blagoev, Nekea	47	Meissner, Charles
50	Blansett, Nora	129	Mendoza, Andrew
38	Blumenthal, Yom Tov	81, 84	Merlin, Bryce
58	Bowman, Dani	61, 86	Miller, Kim
34	Brokaw, Esther	125	Moinicken, Kristen
123	Brokaw, Isabel	64	Nesbitt, Ricky
54	Brown, Susan	98	Nicholson, Nicole
102	Canha, Justin	127, 141	Oberto, Maximus
120	Cantu, Jason	48	Park, Jessica
36	Chwast, Seth	52	Pipoye
126	Clemens, Erin	118	Preboy, Gabriel
75	Cooke, Kevin	71	Randall, Andrew
74	Dawson, Gilbert	33	Raphael, James
116	Deutsch, Marcy	56	Roveta, Craig
27	Doucette, Isabell	134	Sachs, Michael
137	Drucker, Brandon	90	Sargent, Forrest
136	Early, Christian	16	Selpal, Steven
95	Edmond, Sydney	96	Sharp, Tim
88	Erenberg, Noah	29, 44	Smoluk, Ryan
92	Estabrook, Erik	40	Sonalkar, Rohan
124	Florentina	138	Svoboda, Daniel John
18	Gerry-Tucker, Kimberly	4, 100	Tan, J.A.
78	Goad, Grace	106	Thompson, Sarah
114	Grandin, Temple	26	Totire, Natalie
112	Gravino, Amy	60	Vidal, J. Michael
140	Hatton, Carly	122	Waters, Candace
76, 111	Hosseini, Kevin	20	Wood-Robbins, Christopher
104	Iliou, Maria and Athena	130	Williamson, Pamela

ORGANIZATIONS THAT SUPPORT ARTISTS

THE ART OF AUTISM provides a forum for artists, poets and entertainers to express themselves through the website, live shows, film festivals, lectures, and books. Our website is www.the-art-of-autism.com. The organizations below support our book, events, and a common mission in the arts and autism.

ANCA provides international recognition for artists, poets, scientists and creatives on the spectrum through their magazine, website, radio shows, and awards ceremonies. www.naturallyautistic.com

Art Enables located in Washington D.C. is a studio and gallery for emerging artists with developmental disabilities. Artists can sell their art and make an income. www.art-enables.org

Art Walk for Kids/Adults focuses on benefiting artists with special needs and at risk, youth and adults, through a curriculum of art education. Located in Santa Barbara, California. www.artwalkforkids.org

The Autism Highway is a community that raises consciousness about the gifts of autism. They have coloring books and chalk festivals in California. www.autismhwy.com

Autism Movement Therapy provides children with autism a world of fun and exciting sensory/motor experiences. Many locations across the United States. www.autismmovementtherapy.com

Autistic Services, Inc. gives people with autism the opportunity to get involved in the visual and performing arts. Located in Williamsville, New York. www.autisticservices.com

Awe in Autism provides inspiration and encouragement to those affected by autism. They do this through live shows and their website www.aweinautism.org.

The Good Purpose Gallery displays art by professionals who embrace the mission of the Student Education Development Fund (SEDF). Located in Lee, Massachusetts. www.sedfund.org

HeART of the Spectrum Autistic Community Center is an art gallery and art mentoring program that fosters independence, expression, and recognition through creativity. Located in Seattle, Washington. www.theheartofthespectrum.com

JSDD's Wellness, Arts Enrichment (WAE) Center's Art Access Program offers programs such as writing, poetry, and painting. Located in Lyndhurst, New Jersey. www.waecenter.org

KindTree serves and celebrates people on the spectrum through art, recreation, and community. They offer a variety of opportunities for artists around the globe. Located in Eugene, Oregon. www.kindtree.org

The Miracle Project enables children and teens with special needs to express themselves through music, dance, acting, story, and writing. Locations in California and New York. www.themiracleproject.org

Powerlight Studios founded by teenager on the spectrum, gives opportunities to autistic animators and illustrators. www.powerlight-studios.com

Pure Vision Arts (PVA) studio provides an environment that facilitates the opportunity for socialization, sharing of ideas and peer mentoring while working in a supportive atmosphere. Located in Manhattan, NYC. www.purevisionarts.org

Strokes of Genius purpose is to educate and empower individuals with Autism Spectrum Disorders (ASD) by promoting their artistic abilities. www.rcmautismnotebook.com

The Studio at Living Opportunities provides workshops, instruction, and events to promote independence, individuality, creativity and income. Located in Medford, Oregon. www.livingopps.org